Bert Sugar's PUNCHLINES

D0873082

Bert Sugar's PUNCHLINES

The Best of Boxing's Most Colorful Writer

BERT RANDOLPH SUGAR

EDITED BY TOM MCCARTHY

LYONS PRESS
Guilford, Connecticut
An imprint of Lyons Press

Lyons Press is an imprint of Globe Pequot Press.

Project editor: Meredith Dias
Text design/layout: Sheryl P. Kober

Library of Congress Cataloging-in-Publication Data is available on file.

ISBN 978-0-7627-9469-0

Printed in the United States of America

10 9 8 7 6 5 4 3 2 1

CONTENTS

FOREWORD

By George Willis, *The New York Post*

For me it was the pants. Sure, everyone knew Bert Sugar for his fedora, the ever-present hat on his head that made him instantly recognizable to anyone who followed boxing. The pants told you more about Bert than the hat. They were oppressively loud: orange, red, or blue. They were sometimes patched with cartoon faces or some other silly designs.

Those pants could have easily passed for pajamas, yet they told you Bert Sugar was his own brand long before the term became fashionable. The hat, the pants, his ever-present cigar, and his relentless quest for a corny joke all made him one of the most unique characters of our time.

I don't remember exactly the first time I met Bert. I'm sure our friendship was cemented over a cocktail in Las Vegas, Memphis, Los Angeles, or the site of some other big boxing event.

Bert was never picky about his audience on any given night. The only prerequisite needed to share his space was a pulse and patience. Bert could talk as easily to a leggy blonde as he could a potbellied boxing fan from Toledo. All they had to do was pretend to listen.

All the better if it was a new friend. They were fresh meat for the one-liners and bad jokes he had repeated too often to others. His garb and his gab often overshadowed his brilliance. He earned a law degree from Michigan and would slip in political commentary in between jokes. Most of all he was humble, often making himself the target of his wisecracks.

He once signed a book for me with the following inscription: "To George, who is still trying to buy back his introduction to . . . Bert R. Sugar."

Being a funny-man was his nature. It was his answer to those who took themselves too seriously. But his humor was not his gift. It was his words, written and spoken, that gave life to boxing's past and present. He may have never thrown a punch in the ring, but Bert Sugar represented boxing as much as any fighter this side of Muhammad Ali.

He was the pioneer of sports-specific reporting, the go-to guy for boxing commentary long before sports talk radio and the Internet sought out experts. Using his dry wit and impeccable insight, Bert could break down any matchup and offer as much inside information as those in the ring.

He wrote books as often as most people send e-mails. They weren't all literary treasures. But they most always made you think, debate, or laugh. He wrote about baseball, thoroughbred racing, and other interests. But he was the heavyweight champion of boxing journalism, the mug shot that defines boxing historian.

If you were fortunate to share a drink with Bert, it was like you were linked to Jack Johnson, Henry Armstrong, Sugar Ray Robinson, Archie Moore, and Ali. He wrote about and ranked *Boxing's Greatest Fighters,* so you figured he had seen them all.

He lived life his way and never looked to his corner for help. You knew Bert Randolph Sugar would run, not walk, through the finish line of life. He wasn't about to watch someone else have all the fun. If Bert wasn't the life of the party, there was no party without his punchlines.

INTRODUCTION

Hanging around Bert Sugar, even for five minutes, could be exhausting if you weren't mentally fit and alert. He talked almost nonstop, like an AK-47 of one-liners, ad libs, and rare historical factoids.

The man was a fountain of knowledge about a lot of things, not just boxing or sports, though that's how he made his living. But the truly wonderful thing about Bert is that he was a good listener, a rare trait in guys like that.

Having lunch or a drink with Bert was an experience anyone would be unlikely to forget. He was, as many of his many obituaries mentioned prominently, encyclopedic in his knowledge, not just of boxing, but of many things—sports, history, politics, art, you name it. He was eminently comfortable discussing anything and everything. But the experience could also be exhausting, because the guy just couldn't stop his constant stream of one-liners, even mid-meal. An hour of two with Bert would be enlightening, certainly entertaining, interesting, and stimulating—sort of a combination of eating with maybe an erudite college professor and Henny Youngman.

Take, for example, a February lunch I had with Bert in a staid old restaurant on the very New Englandy Connecticut shoreline—not exactly the very popular summer place's peak time. The only people eating that afternoon were a group of very old gentlemen at a long table in front of a fireplace.

Bert looked at them and said, "Geez, the average age in here is like . . . dead."

We went on to eat, and Bert was rambling away in his usual entertaining fashion, barely taking a breath between bites, and one of the elderly gentlemen at the other table fell from his chair. His friends and the staff rushed to help, but the man was soon removed on a stretcher by the local ambulance crew.

Bert continued talking during the emergency about other things, but as the EMTs wheeled the man by us, he put down his fork and said, "See, I told you."

Another time, when I was walking with Bert in Manhattan outside the Algonquin, a cabbie, spying Bert, leaned out his window and pounded the side of the door. "*Sugaaaaah!*" was all we could hear as he drove past.

"My people," Bert said drolly as he continued walking.

And he could be sometimes surprising in his varied interests. He played rugby for the University of Michigan Old Boys into his dotage, and I often wondered if he took off his hat or put out his cigar to bind into a scrum.

In earlier days, just out of law school, he worked for an advertising firm in New York and came up with the "*N-E-S-T-L-E-S, Nestles makes the very best, chooooocccooooolllaaaate!!!*" jingle. I would have loved to have seen him in a cameo on *Mad Men*.

You definitely had to bring your A-game or you'd be left behind.

For all his self-deprecation and superficial gruffness, he was a truly perceptive and widely read intellectual, though I suspect he would cringe at even the thought of being called that.

And for all his eccentricities (no cell phone; no e-mail; no computers, just a typewriter), Bert was, more than anything, a serious writer.

After Bert's death in 2012, the obituaries and tributes flowed from around the world.

Take this from Allen Barra in *The Atlantic:*

If Bert Sugar—the boxing writer and historian who died Sunday at age 75 of cardiac arrest following a long bout with lung cancer—had never existed, God would have had a hard time inventing him. He'd have needed help from Ring Lardner, Damon Runyan [sic], and A.J. Liebling. And even when they were done, they'd need a strong assist from Bert himself, who came as close as anyone I've ever known to creating a character for himself and then living it.

Or this from Beau Denison on SportsPageMagazine.com:

Bert Sugar not only set a standard for sports writers, he raised the bar so high that those of us who follow are merely playing for second. He was the best of us.

When I began writing and struggling to find my way, in doing research for a column, I came across an editorial written by Bert Sugar. I was instantly captivated and found myself reading it over and over. It was as though he reached out of the paper, grabbed me by the ears, and said: "Read and Learn Son, Read and Learn." He had a profound impact on me and became an instant inspiration to strive for perfection.

It is no wonder Mr. Sugar was called "The Greatest Boxing Writer of the 20th Century" by the International Veteran Boxing Association.

And it's no wonder the most difficult, even painful, part of compiling this volume was deciding what pieces of Bert Sugar's wonderful boxing writing *not* to use.

SUGAR ON HIS CRITICS

I Didn't Know Writing Was a Contact Sport

Last May 15th, the following story appeared in *The New York Daily News* under the headline, "Toughs Leave Bert Sugar Feeling Beat":

"Two thugs entered the West 43rd St. offices of *Boxing Illustrated* yesterday and punched the magazine's illustrious publisher and editor, Bert Sugar, who seemed more perplexed than hurt. 'I've been hit harder,' said Sugar, 'but I'm justifiably peeved. If this was a message, who was it from? The detectives asked me if anybody had a grudge against me. I said, "How long do you have?" All I know, these two guys, about 25, came in, one cut my telephone lines and the other hit me twice and missed a third punch.' The worst thing, Sugar said, was the hoods knocked off his ubiquitous hat. Anyone with information as to the assailants will probably be given a medal."

Wasted Efforts

And what have my efforts begotten me? Along the way I've been sued, screwed and tattoo'd—the latter by two thugs who obviously didn't much care for what I had written and broke into my office to render their complaint with their fists, although I would much preferred that they had communicated their dissatisfaction via Western Union. I also have been the recipient of death threats, serial phone harassment and more than enough "loving" reviews of my character by those who have reacted as if I had just pointed out a case of hoof and mouth disease in a personal favorite of theirs in the herd to fill an oversized scrapbook.

Faulty Logic

So, gentlemen, start your arguing. All over again. And once more you can attack me for my reasoning like a man who thinks his wife has stopped smoking cigarettes just because he found cigar butts in her ashtray. But I stand by it. That is, until next time . . .

What of It?

Believing all along that the faint of heart never won so much as a scrap of paper, I have picked many scraps—sometimes taking on both sides. Or, as Allen Barra of *The Wall Street Journal* once wrote, "Bert Randolph Sugar will argue about anything at the drop of a hat and have a contrary opinion before the hat hits the floor."

Wepner Weighs In

Chuck Wepner, dubbed "the Bayonne Bleeder" because of his propensity to bleed—usually somewhere between "Oh, Say . . ." and "Can You See . . ."—stood at the rostrum at a Friar's Club jolly-hop smelling blood. Only this time it wasn't his; it was mine. Extending his massive arm, which had the effect of making him look like a railroad crossing, he pointed in my direction and, in a voice sounding like he had just gnarled ground glass, said, "Some people say Bert Sugar is disgusting, obnoxious, and revolting. I say they're wrong. Bert Sugar is revolting, obnoxious, and disgusting."

Nice of You to Say

Take Chris Jones's description of me in his book Falling Hard: "The veteran writer and boxing historian has one of the sport's most recognizable mugs. He's somewhere between sixty and one hundred years old. He's as bald as a coot and wears a fedora to cover his dome. His eyes are sunken behind a bulbous nose, and a cigar is forever stuffed into his black, wet mouth. Sugar wears clothes that match his outdated personality. Doesn't talk so much as bark."

All Man

Nik Cohn, in his book, *Heart of the World,* not only seconds the emotion but raises it several levels, describing me as "A large, wet man, his face all mouth and bloodshot eyes, he was possessed of great hungers, even greater thirsts, and his acts are scaled to match."

Big Mouth

Frank Prial of *The New York Times:* "(Sugar) is an old-time hard drinking wise-cracking newsman . . . Sugar's signature fedora, with a wide 1930s brim, framed a high forehead and long, animated face and mouth that, it soon became evident, rarely closed."

Prince Harming

Ira Berkow of *The New York Times* called me "Boxing's Thucydides," Al Silverman of *Sport* magazine, "the long-time Pericles of boxing," and Rob Ryan of *The Boston Globe,* "one of sport's greatest living historians"—but so-called rave reviews could easily fit on a postcard crowded with a description of the view on the obverse side and with more than enough room left for an address and an oversized postage stamp. Granted, I was never in the running for "Prom King," but how did I wind up being subject to soaking up so many stones thrown in my direction? What was it that made me more Prince Harming than Charming?

SUGAR EXPLAINS HIMSELF

His Career

It's been one helluva ride and I wouldn't trade it for anything, the most fun I've ever had with my clothes on.

His Slight Cynicism

Tracing the breadcrumbs all the way back, the moment when I first showed signs of going "askew" came when, as a young paperboy in Washington, D.C., I chanced to find myself knocking on the door of one of the subscribers on my route, someone identified in my collection book only as a "Mr. McAuliffe." But when the door was opened, what to my wondering eyes should appear but a man bedecked in enough medals to start a scrap metal drive. Stuttering sounds that made an attempt at words, I spat forth something that sounded like, "Are you the General McAuliffe who said 'Nuts!' at the Battle of the Bulge?" Or somesuch. To which he merely said, "No . . . I said 'Fuck 'em!' . . ." And with that, he slammed the door. That was when I first realized that not only was truth the first casualty of war, but that what I read came as close to the truth as calling a myth a female moth.

Self-Deprecation

There is no truth to the rumor that I covered Cain vs. Abel. I mean, I was there, but I just couldn't get credentials. At my age, old age is defined as being fifteen years older than whatever I am.

The Good Life

Having graduated law school—if finishing 313th in a class of 313 can be called "graduating"—and passing the bar, which was the only bar I ever passed, I came to New York, ambition in mind and résumé in hand. I also came away with a tremendous headache. As well as the belief that writers subscribe to the theorem that being a good liver is better than having one.

Influences

The scales fell from my eyes and I suddenly became aware of writers like H.L. Mencken who saw things as they were, not as they ought to be. Then it was on to Ambrose Bierce, Oscar Wilde, Ring Lardner, Damon Runyon and others who, almost as if smelling flowers, began to look around for the coffin, trafficked in the same unpleasant way of telling the truth, their writings crackling with wit and barbed-wire irony—called "cynicism" by those who didn't understand truth when they saw it.

A Good Thing about Joe Louis

The bar was an important part of every writer's road map, even Red Smith, who always ordered his drinks, "No fruit, please." Making a note of it in one of his columns on Joe Louis: "Joe Louis was a newspaperman's champion. He always finished in time for the first edition so us guys could get our stories done and make it to the bar with hours to go before closing time."

Bugs Baer, My Hero

The drinking went on and on and on . . . almost as if those at the bar had found drinks so ill they had to stay up half the night to tend to them. And with the drinks went the stories.

One I remember had to do with a newspaperman named Bugs Baer, who had written for the old *Journal-American* back in the '20s and '30s. Baer had penned such memorable lines as the one about a ballplayer he described as having "the greatest day since Lizzie Borden went 2-for-2 in Fall River, Massachusetts." Or another, this one on Fred Fulton, who had been KO'd by Jack Dempsey in seconds: "He could sell advertising space on the soles of his shoes."

Cwhris Schenkel?

If the truth be known, the sound of Chris Schenkel's voice is enough to launch a "Bring Back Howard Cosell" campaign.

What's with the Hat?

Why the trademark hat? Oh, and another thing I learned in my introductory course at Toots U. was that hats were more than merely an article worn to conceal the shape of a newspaperman's head. As some of the older writers would have it, hats were part and parcel of every newspaperman's protective gear, sitting as they did on the floor below the early linotype machines which rained a steady stream of hot type down on their heads from above through ill-fitting floor boards. The practice of protecting their heads was so prevalent that when Ben Hecht and Charles MacArthur wrote their popular play "Front Page," they made sure every newspaperman in their script came adorned with a hat, worn inside and out.

What about the Cigar?

And the cigar? How did that become part and parcel of a young writer? Trying to sort through the dual manipulations of time and memory as best I can, maybe I took up cigars because of a talk given by Walt Kelly, the creator of that wonderful comic strip Pogo, who said that "the ability to twirl a cigar as a youngster gave the young manipulator a sense of freedom and courage." Or maybe it was because Knobby Walsh, the manager of the comic-strip character Joe Palooka, always had a cigar as a go-with his hat and I thought it was part of the boxing scene. But whatever it was, I adopted the cigar and the lifestyle that supposedly went with it—although by the time I reached a certain age the cigar gave me something to hold on to in case I was falling down.

Future Plans

Please take down the effigies hung in my honor and sheath your knives. For you will continue to find me at every big fight, seated there at ringside. You'll recognize me, just look for the snap-brimmed hat, the cigar and "the clothes that match his outdated personality" and "the Godzilla roar . . ." Oh, never mind!

Guiding Stars

Take Ring Lardner's line: "The America's Cup is as exciting as watching grass grow." Or Red Smith's on Primo Carnera: "the world's most beautiful, most ferocious and most talented heavyweight champion in the era between Jack Sharkey and Max Baer." Or Jim Murray's on the Indy 500: "Gentlemen, start your hearses." Et cetera, etc., etc., the et ceteras going on for about five pages or more. As a young cynic-in-training, these writers, and their lines, became my guiding star.

Bugs Baer, Redux

Anyway, the story went that one day Baer was sitting at his desk writing his column when a fight manager chanced to come in with his fighter in tow. Trying to sell Bugs a column, he said, "Bugs, meet the heavyweight champion of South Africa." "Who let you in?" demanded Bugs. "Sorry, can't talk to you now, I'm busy . . . some other time, maybe . . ." But the manager was persistent. "Bugs, really, this is the champion of South Africa . . . Would make a good story . . ." Baer again dismissed him, "Sorry, too busy . . ." Still the manager went on his merry, "Bugs, you ought to meet this kid . . . he's the champion of South Africa . . ." With that Bugs looked up from his typewriter for the first time and, getting up, threw one of the most pluperfect right hands even seen, in or out of the ring, nailing the so-called "Champion of South Africa" square on the puss, knocking him down in a heap. "Now I'm the champion of South Africa," said Baer, who sat down and went back to typing his column.

Why Boxing?

I had no idea which sport I wanted to write about. Here, like Roy Campanella, who, when asked by his high school coach to take the position he wanted to play along with other hopefuls, ran to the outfield and found seventy other kids in left, eighty in center and ninety in right and nobody behind home plate and decided at that moment to become a catcher, I found seventy writers in left covering basketball, eighty in center football, ninety in right baseball, and nobody behind home plate covering boxing. So, like Campanella, as fast as I could get there, I became a boxing writer, buying a publication called *Boxing Illustrated*.

The Best

Boxing has many, many redeeming factors. I had the chance to meet some of the most interesting people in the world of sports, if not the world, period—writers like Eddie Schuyler, Bob Waters, Pat Putnam, Phil Berger, Jon Saraceno, Budd Schulberg, Jim Murray, Thom Loverro, Sam Skinner, Barney Nagler, Mike Katz, John Phillips, Wally Matthews and many more; or managers and trainers like Ray Arcel, Angelo Dundee, Manny Steward, Lou Duva, Teddy Atlas and so many others; or the reason for the sport, the fighters themselves, like Muhammad Ali, Larry Holmes, Tommy Hearns, Joe Frazier, Marvelous Marvin Hagler, Archie Moore, Roberto Duran, Ray Leonard, Sugar Ray Robinson (there being only one Sugar Ray!), Willie Pep, Jose Torres, Gerry Cooney and too many more to acknowledge in this small space. Or appear in "cameos" in four movies, all of which won for me Worst Supporting Actor awards.

SPRINKLED SUGAR

The Once-Greats of Boxing Should Sit

Why are so many once-great stars still attempting to ply *their* trade? Could it be they've got nowhere else to go. Or just that they've missed the adulation of the crowds. Or perhaps it's just that time-honored answer: money. Whatever it is, boxing has taken on a new glow, and it ain't a healthy one as more and more of the once-great climb through the ropes to let us watch the gilt of their once-greatness peel off before our very eyes.

Really?

Bribery going on in boxing? I almost felt like Claude Rains in *Casablanca* when Humphrey Bogart handed him his gambling winnings and he said, tongue firmly wedged in cheek, "I'm shocked . . . Shocked! to know that gambling goes on here, Rick."

On Certain Celebrities

Toots Shor's was the saloon where the New York sporting crowd hung out for the meat of the last century, a bar for guys' guys, as much an altar as a bar, catering to those who wished to be seen and obscene, the writers, the athletes and anyone who was anyone, or wished they were. It was always crowded to the gunwales, as it had been the night Charlie Chaplin, nervously waiting for a table, complained to Toots about the need to stand on line. To which Toots, paying him no-never-mind, merely shouted over his shoulder, "Just stand there and be funny, Charlie," leaving the world's funniest man—who was not in a funny mood at the moment—still waiting on line, although not very still.

A Shot for Fleming?

Another time, Toots, who was partial to athletes, especially those from New York, found himself talking to Sir Alexander Fleming, the inventor of penicillin. Not exactly sure who he was talking to or why and trying to make polite conversation—which didn't come easily to Toots, an old-time salooniere whose dialogue was peppered with a cheerful contempt for the English language and salted with more than a few words like "Crumbbum." Toots was overjoyed to be interrupted by one of his retainers informing him that Mel Ott, the then-manager of the New York baseball Giants, had just arrived. Glad to be rescued from his uncomfortable situation, Toots merely gave a Toots-a-loo and an "Excuse me, someone important just came in," and left Sir Alexander there to molder.

What It Means

What boxing has meant down through the ages is that it is a sport that has given many of us heart, hope and heroes.

In Defense of Boxing

There is some medical evidence that shows boxing is like cigarettes, dangerous to the health. But even the A.M.A. ranks boxing seventh in terms of deaths per thousand participants, behind such establishment sports as football and auto racing. But the A.M.A., like any other lobbying group, knows better than to take on another well-entrenched lobbying group.

On Boxing's Dubious State

It was almost as much a thrill to read about the federal indictment of the International Boxing Federation as it was to read *Fortune* magazine and find out that the heads of the IBF are among the dozen richest men in the country.

Judging a Fighter

A fighter's greatness should be judged like a properly ripened fruit, at the peak of picking, not before and certainly not after, but at that magic moment of greatness.

The Weight of History

Having spent countless hours listening to those whose recollections go all the way back to sometime just after the Great Flood, it is important to know when to cherish their memories without actually embracing them and accept them along generational fault lines. For truth be told, while one must take stock of the inventory that went before, they must also take into account those who fought in more recent times and whose exploits not only compare favorably with such old timers, but oft-times dwarf them.

On Arguing

Controversy to boxing is like an olive garnish to a martini, enlivening it.

On Women's Boxing

While the ink-stained wretches of the press corps, with all the ardor of astronomers discovering a new star in the chorus of galaxies, are wearing their pencils down to stubs chronicling women's boxing, I, for one, am having great difficulty accepting it as a sport.

Trying to explain my position expansively, if not plausibly—possibly because little about it is plausible—I believe it must have something to do with the feminist movement; somewhat along the lines of the song *Anything You Can Do, I Can Do Better.* But, then again, I've always thought that women who wanted to be the equal of men have no ambition.

On British Fighters

It was Red Smith, the poet laureate of all sportswriters, who penned the immortal lines ". . . the deep, dreamless slumber that comes to small children, the pure of heart, and all British heavyweights."

Incurable British boxing fans have always taken great nourishment in those few small accomplishments of their heavies, with memories of Tommy Farr's going fifteen rounds with Joe Louis, 'Enery Cooper knocking down then-Cassius Clay and Frank Bruno momentarily stunning Mike Tyson all dancing in their heads. After all, it's part and parcel of the British mentality to instinctively admire any man who can make defeat sound like a victory. (Don't forget, they view Dunkirk as a victory.)

On Tex Cobb

It was a fight so one-sided that Cobb, who couldn't have caught Holmes with the aid of a taxi cab, at one point threw up his hands and, turning to referee Steve Crossen, hollered, "You're white, help me!"

Women's Boxing: Part II

I'd rather poke my eye out with a sharp stick than watch women's boxing! Oh sure, women have the right to fight, just as men have the right to do "The Full Monty." But I also retain some rights, such as the right not to watch. As far as I'm concerned, the best fight between women I ever saw was the one between Marlene Dietrich and Una Merkle in the movie *Destry Rides Again,* with a lot of hair-pulling and rolling around in the dust.

On Howard Cosell

Howard, who belongs to that long line of sportscasters who have tried to write—and who, according to his editor, the late Ed Kuhn, had difficulty putting two words together—should remember what his function in his life has been: A purveyor of amusement for people who do not have sufficient wit to amuse themselves. To call himself a "Journalist," or anything else for that matter, is intellectually dishonest. But what else can you expect from a man who continues to say he "Tells it *LIKE* it is," when good English and William Shakespeare would suggest that the line should be "Tells it *AS* it is."

Boycotting Mike Tyson

When it comes to the Lennox Lewis/Mike Tyson fight on June 8 in Memphis, in the immortal words of film mogul Samuel Goldwyn, "Include me out."

I'm boycotting the fight because of my love for the sport and what Mike Tyson has done to demean it. For, in the strangest association since Professor Rorschach toppled over his inkwell, Mike Tyson has become, in the public's mind, the poster boy for boxing, even though he is less representative of the sport than Dracula is for the Red Cross's annual blood drive.

The Boxing Myth

The other group to come forward—and against boxing at the same time—is some group of do-gooders called "The National Coalition on Television Violence." Their ranks include several activists from previous wars, including the heads of such organizations as "Bothered about Dungeons & Dragons," "Women Against Pornography," and other such pressing issues of the day who have now dragged their soap boxes over to boxing's corner of the street. In a press release they "reveal" their findings that "New Research Confirms Boxing Promotes Aggression" and "protest the presence of boxing at the Olympic Games." Great! These idiots in idiots' clothing would have you believe, as it says in their press release, that because "brawls broke out in the boxing arena at both the 1987 Pan-American Games and at the 1988 Olympic Games," the sport should be banned. Have they ever looked at the rioting at soccer games in Europe? Do they advocate banning soccer?

The Hope of Boxing

To understand boxing one must understand its roots. From its beginnings, the sport has resonated with urban ethnicity, drawing its recruits from the tenements, the ghettos, the projects, the barrios, the "nabes," places that offered little presence and even less of a future.

What Boxing Means

Traditionally, boxing has been the sport of the dispossessed, their social staircase for entering the mainstream of society. Before the turn of the century, when signs in Boston's windows read, "NINA," for "No Irish Need Apply," a young man named John L. Sullivan turned to boxing and became America's first great sports hero.

The Culprits

For although boxing is a sport in its own right, it is also a sport in its own wrong. And the primary culprits are those clowns in clowns' clothing, those sanctioning bodies called "The Alphabets"—shorthand for "The Alphabet Soups," a term I coined as editor of *Ring Magazine* back in the early '80s to describe organizations like the WBC, the WBA and the IBF, all dedicated to the belief that you can fool too many people too much of the time.

THE CLASSIC FIGHTS

Rocky Marciano vs. Jersey Joe Walcott
Philadelphia Stadium, Philadelphia, Pennsylvania
September 23, 1952

With one deep-dish beauty of a right at forty-three seconds into the thirteenth round, Rocky Marciano almost tore the head off defending champion Jersey Joe Walcott, knocking off his crown in the process—a crown he had worn securely for the previous twelve rounds.

It was a right hand that traveled no more than six inches, and yet it reached back seventy years, to the first modern heavyweight, "Boston Strongboy" John L. Sullivan. And with it, Marciano became not only the first heavyweight champion to come from the same area as Sullivan, but the first man to ascend to the throne with a perfect record since Sullivan had accomplished the same feat seven decades before.

For twelve rounds the so-called Brockton Blockbuster had hardly seemed like the world-beater the betting society had thought he was when they made him a 9–5 favorite. The same firepower that had ended the career of Joe Louis, stopped Harry ("Kid") Matthews in two, and sent Carmen Vingo to the hospital, was totally ineffective in stopping Jersey Joe—or Father Time, Walcott's greatest ally.

Right from the opening bell, Walcott made a liar out of the naysayers who said that he was too old and "the Rock" too much for the champ. Throwing his powerful left hook—the same left hook that had taken out Ezzard Charles just the previous year and decked Joe Louis three times—Walcott floored Marciano midway through the first round, the first time in his 43-fight professional career that Rocky had ever been down. Up at the count of four ("I got up fast because I was more mad at myself than hurt," Marciano was to say later), he looked hurt. Eschewing his patented shuffle, the 198-pound Walcott went right back to the attack, swarming all over the 184-pound challenger, staggering him again at the bell.

The second round was more of the same, with Walcott on the attack, even planting a left hook somewhere south of the border of Marciano's beltline, further adding to the challenger's discomfiture.

Rocky, trying to stem the tide of battle and turn the momentum, came out for Round 3 in a deep crouch as his manager, Al Weill, kept up a staccato of "Keep down low, keep down low." But again Walcott found his way through the challenger's defense, landing another clean left to the chin. But despite repeated meetings of his right chin with the champion's left, Marciano showed that even though he lacked polish and finesse, he possessed a chin of granite and a heart to match as he came back to exchange shots with Walcott after the bell.

By Round 6 "the Rock" had taken the battle to Walcott and made him fight his kind of fight, backing the champion into the ropes and blazing away with lefts and rights. During one of their heated exchanges, Marciano suffered a deep gash on his head and

Walcott a cut eyelid. As the bell rang, blood flowed freely from Walcott's damaged left eye and the end looked imminent for the oldest champion ever to defend his crown.

But somehow, someway, somewhere, the solution used to stem the flow of blood (here the story becomes clouded as to whether it was the solution on Marciano's head or Walcott's eye) got into Marciano's eyes. By the end of Round 7 Marciano came back to his corner hollering, "I have trouble with my left eye. I can't see."

[With Rocky] blind for three more rounds, Walcott made the most of them, using everything he knew and threw to beat "the Rock." Marciano missed repeatedly and Walcott countered with his own lefts and rights, cutting Marciano between the eyes and on the forehead.

By the end of the twelfth round Walcott was in total control. Ahead on all three officials' cards (7–4–1, 7–5, and 8–4), all he had to do was "last" nine more minutes. He was to miss by eight minutes and seventeen seconds.

With just thirty seconds gone in the thirteenth round, and with no punches thrown, Walcott unexplainably backed into the ropes. He was caught there with as hard a punch as had ever been seen in a fight—a short right hand that caught him flush coming off the ropes. As a grazing left (thrown for good measure and merely serving as a postscript) swept by him, Walcott slowly sank to the canvas, one arm hanging onto the ring rope, a grotesque imitation of a religious fanatic in prayer. Referee Charley Daggert counted ten over the inert form. He could have counted to 100 for all the difference it made.

Back in his dressing room, where there was more backslapping going on than could be found at a Shriner's convention, the thoroughly exhausted champ greeted his well-wishers while over in one corner his father, Peter Marchegiano, wept. "I'm proud," he said over and over again.

So were many other well-wishers who wouldn't make it into the dressing room, but still crowded into the ring where their favorite son—twenty-six years after Tunney had dethroned Dempsey in the very same ring—had won the title. They had all won. Everyone, that is, except Marciano, who had lost a new pair of trousers in the confusion to some souvenir hunter and had to leave Municipal Stadium with a bathrobe thrown over an incomplete suit.

Jack Dempsey vs. Luis Firpo
Polo Grounds, New York
September 14, 1923

If they had been two bull moose, horns interlocked, fighting for their turf, they would have ground each other into fine dust; if they had been two Roman gladiators, replete with tridents and shields, they would have reduced each other into two puddles that could have been borne off by blotters; and if they had fought on a barge, Luis Angel Firpo would have beaten Jack Dempsey to become the heavyweight champion of the world.

Luis Angel Firpo was a great bull of a man. Dubbed by one less than imaginative writer, "the Wild Bull of the Pampas," this Argentinian stood some six feet, three inches tall and weighed some 220 pounds in the days when heavyweights barely scaled 200. His idea of fighting was simple: hit your opponent with a bludgeoning right hand, period. But his skills, or lack thereof, had gotten noticeable results. He had taken on—and beaten—six men since he had landed on the shores of America some eighteen months before, dispatching all of them in fewer than the scheduled number of rounds. His victims included among their number two whom the heavyweight champion of the world, Jack Dempsey, had also dispensed, Jess Willard and Bill Brennan. And Firpo had needed only four more rounds to do away with them than had Dempsey.

So, it was no wonder that promoter Tex Rickard looked upon this walking version of the Andes as the next logical contender for Jack Dempsey. Especially since Dempsey had just practiced mayhem less on his opponent, Tommy Gibbons, than on the little town of Shelby, Montana in his last fight. And, if memory served Rickard correctly, and it usually did, his last Dempsey fight was a million-dollar one, with another foreigner—in that case, Georges Carpentier—serving as the party of the second part. Rickard couldn't think of a better match than one between Dempsey and Firpo in early fall in New York. But the giant Firpo, who, like many immigrants, had come to America thinking the streets were paved with gold and would break the fingers of anybody around him to get to an idle nickel lying on the sidewalk, knew the worth of a build-up almost as much as he knew the worth of a build. He wasn't about to be rushed into a match with Dempsey, preferring, as he told Rickard in his best English—which also was his worst English, almost nonexistent—that he wanted to wait another year before challenging anyone for the title. Rickard eyed the man before him, dressed in a rumpled $15 suit with a yellowed celluloid collar that would have been discarded months before if it hadn't cost another quarter to buy another, and said, "But next year you may get a lot of money fighting Dempsey. This year, you will get a lot of money." It took no interpreter to tell Firpo what to do. He signed, thereby becoming the first Latin American ever to challenge for a world's title.

But even if Luis Firpo had impressed his victims with his might, Rickard's move had not impressed the New York media as right. One columnist was moved to write, "Has Rickard run out of common sense, as well as contenders? Firpo, without question, is the clumsiest-looking oaf ever proposed as a challenger to a heavyweight champion." The oddsmakers concurred, installing Dempsey—in this, his fourth title defense—as an overwhelming 3–1 favorite.

However, a sports-starved public viewed the battle as a battle of giants and paid no heed to disproportionate odds or a disparaging press, thronging to the Polo Grounds the day of the fight for tickets. With a larger army on hand than Gallieni had led out of Paris to the first battle of the Marne, some 125,000 fans, believing that, like nature, Rickard abhorred a vacuum, tried to fill 82,000 seats. It was a classic case of demand far outstripping supply. In those pre-ERA days, a woman headed the long grey line of people pushing to get general admission tickets. However, despite her long vigil, when push came to shove and the line was broken up by a frantic mob seeking to get the bleacher seats, she lost her place. When the line was reassembled and the tickets actually were placed on sale, the crush of the crowd was so great that she was somewhere on the outskirts of the crowd, unable to get within half a block of the ticket window.

Still, some 85,000 fans came in through the gates, over and under the turnstiles, and even over the fence, to fill the 82,000 seats and give Rickard another million-dollar-plus gate, paying $1,188,603 for the privilege of seeing two men beat the living whey out of each other. They overflowed the aisles, stood on seats and gave little ground to those seeking their rightful seats, especially in the $50 ringside section. The only time the sea of humanity parted was when the two combatants coursed down from their centerfield dressing rooms to be greeted by rousing cheers. It was a crescendo that was never to subside.

Standing in the middle of the ring to receive their instructions from referee Jack Gallagher, the difference in size could be seen. There was a 24-pound difference in their weights, Firpo weighing in at 216½, Dempsey at 192½. But their size differential was measured in more than mere weight, for Firpo stood almost three inches taller than the champion, and his primitive musculature made the champion seem puny by comparison. As referee Gallagher intoned the instructions, an interpreter stood at Firpo's side. But even an interpreter couldn't have given voice to two instructions that never were uttered, two instructions which could have changed the course of the heavyweight division: that upon scoring a knockdown a man must go to the furthest neutral corner; and that a man knocked from the ring must get back in within ten seconds under his own power.

Then there was the bell, seemingly lost in the continuous cataract of sound which 82,000 voices made. Firpo came out in an unusual stance, for him. It was the classic boxer stance, taught him by his American trainer, Jimmy DeForest, who had tried to instill in this South American Neanderthal, who knew absolutely nothing about the science of self-defense—his only defense being his right fist—a modicum of science.

Dempsey crouched low, all the better to appraise the giant in front of him and minimize his target. But the champion didn't get much of an opportunity to assess Firpo or his moves. For Firpo's first punch was a thunderous—and ponderous—right which caught Dempsey on the jaw, sending him to the canvas only ten seconds into the fight.

Dempsey jumped off the canvas with no count, more embarrassed by being knocked off-balance than hurt, and went to the attack. As the two flailing behemoths' arms entangled, they fell into a clinch. The referee shouted "break" and, as the trusting Firpo dropped his hands and glanced inquiringly at the ref, Dempsey threw a left hook over Firpo's half held-up right. It landed on the jaw and now Firpo was down. He, too, was up without a count. The first two punches had produced two knockdowns, both all within twenty seconds. It was to set a record. And a pattern. For as soon as Firpo had bounced up, he threw himself into the champion, connecting with a right to the only spot available to him, Dempsey's body. Dempsey continued to sacrifice his body, holding his hands high up, against his chin and against the chance that Firpo would land another of his lethal rights. But Firpo paid Dempsey no mind, just as he had paid no attention to advice from his handlers, and threw another looping right which came from somewhere out in right field. It caught the champion on the point of the jaw. But this time, instead of finding refuge on the canvas—as he had from the first right—Dempsey instead found refuge in returning firepower with firepower, drilling a left uppercut through Firpo's haphazard defense. The Argentinian stood there wavering. Then, with a resounding thud, he crashed to the canvas for the second time.

As the crowd jumped to its feet, yelling, screaming, climbing up on the benches, falling down, clawing at each other, roaring forth a wild, tumultuous cascade of sound in the greatest sustained mass audience-hysteria ever witnessed, Firpo, too, tried to jump up. But Dempsey, like an avenging angel, stood over him, ready to jump on the man as soon as his hands left the resin of the canvas. As they did, Dempsey caught him with a left and a right. But instead of retreating, Firpo came on, throwing three devastating hammer rights into Dempsey's unguarded rib cage. Then, as he sought to bring off yet another booming right to the body, Dempsey stepped instead with his own bomb, a left hook to the chin. Firpo fell as if he had been poleaxed, flat on his face, arms surrounding his head.

Miraculously he arose, only to run into Dempsey who had positioned himself directly over the head of the fallen challenger. Dempsey was off target with a right, grazing Firpo's head. But Firpo was so groggy that its force brushed him back to the canvas for the fourth time. The referee tried to push Dempsey away. As he backed up, Firpo got up. Dempsey was back on him faster than you can say Luis Angel Firpo, and, after another left and right to the jaw, Luis Angel Firpo was back where he had begun that exchange—on the floor. This time, after righting himself, Firpo found Dempsey waiting for him the very second his hands had tentatively cleared the floor. Another right sent Firpo down for the sixth time in the round.

Somehow, either from resolution or instinct, Firpo got to his feet, shaking but still trying to hurl just one of his rights at the onrushing Dempsey to turn the tide of battle. But before he wound up to throw it a left and a right from Dempsey floored the Argentine giant a seventh time. This time he looked like he was through, his head buried in the mat, his arms stretched out. But unbelievably the giant shook, shivered and then stood up, reaching a standing posture just before the fatal count of "10."

Now, calling on some superhuman effort, Firpo flung himself at Dempsey, bullying him away from him, across the ring. Then, with Dempsey on the retreat, the battle-blind and berserk Firpo threw a clubbing right which landed aside Dempsey's head and the champion, impaled on the ropes, proved Newton's Law—that every action has an opposite and equal reaction—by falling through the ropes into the press section, feet flying and with his arms behind him to cushion his fall. It was the most famous moment in sports, captured for all time by George Bellows's equally famous portrait. In the words of Bugs Baer, Dempsey had "skipped three ropes at once." Somehow, in a stadium where Rickard had built the press benches higher than usual, fate conspired to have Dempsey fall on the typewriter of Jack Lawrence of the *New York Tribune,* who was more worried about protecting the forty-four keys of his typewriter than the 192½ pounds of falling champion. But whatever the reason, the result was the same; Lawrence hydraulically jacked the champ up onto the ring apron by the count of seven. By the count of eight Dempsey could be seen by a handful of people struggling up onto the ring apron. And by nine he had climbed between the middle and lower ropes and was back in the ring.

The rest of the round found Firpo literally hurling right hands at Dempsey, who instinctively rolled slightly under the punches, breaking their force. Had Firpo even had a hint of a left hand, the championship would have changed hands. But such was not the case, and he spent the remainder of Round 1 taking aim at the bobbing head in front of him with an unvaried nonassortment of right-hand swings. The end of the round found Dempsey still on his feet, beginning to throw punches of his own. Even after the bell he threw several punches at Firpo, all of which landed, leaving both men dazed and spent from their first-round efforts.

The bell for Round 2 had scarcely sounded when Dempsey picked up where he had left off, throwing short inside punches and taking rights to the body. Dempsey, hurt slightly by one of Firpo's rib-crackers, fell into a clinch. Then, on the break, he stepped back in and began throwing combinations to Firpo's head. Two left hooks landed over Firpo's by-now limp guard. A left to the body, followed by two right uppercuts and another left to the body. Firpo tried to hold on, but Dempsey pulled away and caught the exhausted challenger with another left and right to the head. Firpo less fell than wilted to the ground, down for the eighth time. Once more he defied gravity and pulled himself erect at the count of five. He pulled back and clouted Dempsey with a wild right to the neck. Dempsey moved in close and found Firpo with a left to the jaw and followed up with a right, literally lifting the Argentine from his feet and hurling him headlong to the floor with the crashing sound of a mighty oak falling from great heights. Firpo lay on the floor, full-length, his gloves covering his head. As the count progressed he shuddered and turned his body, trying once again to will himself up—to get back into battle. But this time he was not to arise. This time it was over.

It had lasted exactly three minutes and fifty-seven seconds, 237 seconds of mayhem, in which 11 knockdowns were scored in the shortest and wildest "great fight" in the history of boxing. It could hardly be called "The Sweet Science," but it was one helluva sweet quarrel.

Rocky Graziano vs. Tony Zale
Yankee Stadium, New York (September 27, 1946)
Chicago Stadium, Chicago (July 16, 1947)
Ruppert Stadium, Newark, New Jersey (June 10, 1948)
There have been twosomes throughout history that have gone together like salt and pepper. These twosomes have sprung up in every field imaginable: Biblical, Cain and Abel; mythological, Damon and Pythias; musical, Gilbert and Sullivan; comical, Weber and Fields; political, Franklin and Delano, etc. Boxing has its own twosomes. Perhaps one of its famous pairings was that of

Zale and Graziano. Like it says in the song, "Love and Marriage": "You can't have one without the other."

For three years, rivals Tony Zale and Rocky Graziano lit up the skies in the world of boxing with fireworks. And today, a half-century later, their fights are still legendary. They weren't fights, they were wars without survivors.

Their rivalry began the night of September 27, 1946 when Zale, "The Man of Steel," from Gary, Indiana, entered the ring with a record of sixty wins—thirty-six by KO, twelve losses and one draw, plus his middleweight crown—to do battle against Graziano. Rocky, a "Dead End Kid" from New York's Mulberry Bend Ghetto, fought the way he lived, according to the rules of the street, alternately hitting and holding anyone who stood in his way. Graziano had compiled a record of forty-three wins— thirty-two by KO, six losses and five draws, including sensational knockout victories over welterweight champions "Red" Cochrane and Marty Servo the previous year.

In a battle that was more savage than scientific, Zale floored Graziano midway through the first round for a count of four. By the end of the round, however, Zale was on the receiving end of a Graziano bombardment and reeling under the attack. Round 2 saw "The Rock" batter the champion around the ring with rights and lefts to the head, splitting Zale's lip in the process and finally toppling Zale with four successive rights. The bell saved Zale at the count of three and Zale was literally dragged to his corner. In the third, Graziano continued his attack with a maniacal fury, hammering the champion at will. However, Graziano could not finish him. When Zale came out for Round 4, he was amazingly refreshed and began to attack, throwing lefts and rights to the body of Graziano and forcing the challenger to retreat. Early in the fifth, Zale pressed his advantage, concentrating on the body with both hands. Suddenly, Graziano leaped at the champion with a tigerish attack and drove Zale back with rights and lefts to the head. But once again Zale weathered the round and came out for Round 6 renewed in vigor and purpose. Graziano made a final furious attempt to finish off "The Man of Steel," but the tide turned once more as Zale crashed home a thunderous right under Graziano's heart, followed by a left hook to the jaw. Rocky sank to his haunches, unable to catch his breath and was counted out for the first time in his career.

A rematch between the two warriors was a foregone conclusion. Ten months later, on July 16, 1947, the two took part in another seesaw slugfest, this time at Chicago Stadium. Zale immediately took the fight to Graziano, punishing him with a steady body barrage and closing his left eye by the end of Round 1. Zale switched his attack to the head in Round 2, attempting to inflict greater damage to Graziano's injured eye. But by the end of the round Zale was in trouble as Graziano connected with a right to the jaw that straightened up the champion and had him so bewildered that he went to the wrong corner at the bell. In Round 3, Zale split open Graziano's left eye and floored him for no count with another right to the head. He then drove the temporarily blinded Graziano into the ropes for an unanswered volley. Round 4 was more of the same, as Graziano spent more time wiping the blood out of his eye than trying to wipe out Zale— although Zale went to the canvas, more from a slip than a punch. By Round 5, the flow of blood had been stemmed, and Graziano started swinging, connecting with a right to the head that seemed to take the steam out of Zale. The champion took the initiative in the opening seconds of the sixth, but it was short-lived as Graziano threw a right cross and then another right to the jaw that sent Zale reeling. Three more rights sent the champion down for a count of three and when he arose the challenger was all over him, draping him over the middle strand of the ropes and pummeling him at will. The fight was halted at 2:10 of the sixth round, and Rocky Graziano was the new middleweight champion of the world. He won the title on his tremendous punching power, his heart and, as he put it, because "Somebody up there likes me."

The rubber match came eleven months later in Newark, New Jersey—the only one that was filmed. Graziano came in as the prohibitive 12–5 favorite. He went out as the ex-champion. The product of the Gary steel mills came out first—and fast—hooking a left to Graziano's jaw and knocking him down with less than a minute gone. The rest of the first round was all Zale's as he banged home his awesome one-two (a right to the body and a left to the jaw) several times. Round 2 was a carbon copy of Round 1 with Zale pounding home his combination. Then, for a brief moment, Graziano flurried, cutting loose with some of his old ferocity and forcing Zale to retreat. The third round continued where the second had left off and then the roof caved in on Rocky as Tony caught the champion with a left hook that floored him. As Graziano struggled to an unsteady position, using the rope as a crutch, Zale was on him again, determined to end it. He caught Rocky with a rib-crunching right to the ribs and followed it up, in perfect tandem, with a left to the jaw. Graziano went down as if poleaxed, and lay there as referee Paul Cavalier counted out "The Rock" at 1:08 of the third round.

Tony Zale became the first middleweight champion since Stanley Ketchel to regain his title. Somebody "Up There" obviously liked him, too.

Carmen Basilio vs. Sugar Ray Robinson
Yankee Stadium, New York
September 23, 1957

There is an old saying that no man walks so tall as the man who has accomplished something. And yet the man who walked the tallest on the morning of Tuesday, September 24, 1957, was the shorter of the two men who had met the previous night in New York's Yankee Stadium to decide the middleweight championship of the world. In fact, he was perhaps the shortest middleweight champion of all time—Carmen Basilio.

Basilio had accomplished something. He had won the middleweight crown from the incomparable Sugar Ray Robinson in as grueling a contest as had ever been witnessed. And, in doing so, he had become only the second welterweight champion ever to step up in class and win the middleweight title. But it wasn't Basilio's height—or lack of it—that decided the outcome of the fight. That was brought home to him when the two fighters were called to the center of the ring for their prefight instructions by referee Al Berl. Basilio, remembering the moment years later, recalled, "I was five-six-and-a-half. I looked up at Sugar Ray. He was sneering at me, trying to scare me. So I started to laugh. I was laughing so hard that the ref had to stop to see if I was OK."

Carmen was not only OK, he was A-OK, and knew then that, to rephrase an old boxing adage, a good little man could beat a good big man if he had one other element to go with it: determination. And that the Canastota, New York onion farmer had, in abundance.

Basilio discovered early on he needed that determination, for, almost from the sound of the opening bell, Robby began a steady ratta-tat-tat tattoo of left jabs into the readily available face of the challenger. By the time the crouching Basilio—whose crouch emphasized further the size differential even more than the five measurable inches and six measured pounds, 160 to 154—was able to penetrate Robinson's defense for the first time, his craggy features had a slightly pink hue, the result of thirteen direct hits by the champion's left jab.

Basilio was trying to go to the body, force the action, score on any part of Robinson that wasn't protected. But first he had to get past that jab, which kept coming at him with pistonlike efficiency. And when Basilio did get in, Robinson tied him up, his shorter arms in against his sides and holding on until the referee could part them and Sugar could escape back into mid-ring again, away from the bull-like charges of Basilio, away from the pressure Basilio was exerting. Far enough away to start the staccato of jabs all over again. But Robinson, who had gone in as the betting underdog—the fourth time in his last five fights he had been the underdog—looked like anything but an underdog for the first three rounds. This was the man they had called "the greatest pound-for-pound boxer" in the history of boxing, a phrase coined especially for him. And he was jabbing, stabbing, and even grabbing at the rough-hewed features of the man in front of him, beating him both with his punch and to the punch.

In the third round Robinson bloodied Basilio's nose with an uppercut. Then, in the fourth, Robby connected with a right uppercut that cut Basilio's left eye. But still the freshly-stuck bull kept charging at his tormentor, throwing caution to the winds and lefts and rights to the body. Maybe it was his battle plan, or just maybe it was his cornerman, Angelo Dundee, who told the challenger before the start of the fourth round, "Go get him." Whatever, it worked. In the fifth, Basilio began to connect. Not that he hadn't before, but now it was more noticeable, attributable in part to the fact that the 37-year-old Robinson was beginning to wind down, the clock in his elder statesman's body beginning to run on a different time. For the first time Basilio was able to rush Ray into the ropes and land a left-right combination, staying in close and beating the Sugar Man to the punch.

Round 6 was a momentary reprieve for Ray as he once again relied on his stock-in-trade, his left jab, catching the onrushing Basilio on the face with six beautifully timed jabs, moving under and over, countering, bobbing, and weaving. But that was Sugar's last draught of the eternal youth elixir, his last taste of what once was. For the 37-year-old body trapped inside the 20-year-old mind was slowly taking over, slowly dictating the actions and reactions of its owner. And no amount of past greatness could will away the tiredness that now was. Nor the determined challenger. Basilio was now pressing the suddenly slower champion, driving him and the body that had been through 157 ring wars through the hells of an intensive body attack.

Robinson continued to use his jab, but starting in Round 7 he retreated behind it instead of using it as the first part of his vaunted one-two. And the shorter Basilio, disdainful of Robinson's left, kept coming in, throwing hooks, sweeping rights, and even straight right leads, catching Robinson with all of them.

As Round 8 opened, Basilio, his eye now covered with grease coating the cut and looking more like a ghostly apparition than a gladiatorial aspirant, continued to press Robinson, landing with lefts and rights to the body and with left hooks to the head. Occasionally he would vary his attack with a left to the body and a right to the head or a right to the body and another right to the body. But no matter what variation Basilio tried, it worked. Robinson, as was his trademark, would attempt to rally right before the bell in his traditional round-winning flurry, all the better to impress the judges, but to no avail. When he started to attack, more in desperation than in deliberation, Basilio would beat him to the punch.

Rounds 9 and 10 were more of the same. By the tenth Robinson was on his bicycle, trying to move away, to rally his forces for one last-ditch attack. But he was paying for his backward flight as the ever-pressing ex-Marine kept atop him, wading in behind left-rights to the head and to the body.

The eleventh opened as the tenth had ended, with Robinson landing his left and Basilio his right. But this time the positions seemed reversed: it was Robinson landing the heavier blows, looking like he had gone to the well and found new life. Instead of waiting for a round-ending rally, he was carrying the action to Carmen from the beginning—a hard right to the body, another counter-right to the body, a left to the body, and rights and lefts to the body in close as Basilio failed to tie him up. Then, with less than a minute to go in the round, it was Basilio's turn. And what a turn it was. He nailed Sugar on the jaw with three rights, propelling him back to the ropes, and then proceeded to use the champion's head for fungo practice, connecting with a fusillade of punches to the head. It looked like Robinson might go down, but right before the bell he came off the ropes and held.

It was hard for even the most dedicated Robinson fan to see how Robby could come back. His legs were working on a different time basis. His body had been ravaged by Basilio's strafing punches. His best was probably not good enough to hold off the challenger. But in a bout that will be remembered for its eddies and flows, the twelfth was to take another turn, with Robinson turning back the clock, getting in two lefts and a right to the head of the challenger, followed by another left and right—all on target. Suddenly Basilio was on rubbery legs, his balance that of a marionette with its strings cut. One minute he was standing there erect, if not tall, the next he was reeling around the ring looking for a place to fall down. But his Leon Errol act was too good. He wouldn't go down. And at the bell he half-walked, half-staggered back to his corner. And the tired Robinson, having shot his bolt and his best, went wearily back to his.

Still the fireworks weren't over. Robinson set out to finish up where he had left off in the thirteenth, landing an entire series of perfectly punctuated jabs to the now-bloody mess that had once been Basilio's face. It was Carmen who was throwing the desperation punches now; Robinson's were accurate and on target. But just as Robinson seemed to have stemmed the tide, back came Basilio with a vicious right to the jaw that shook Ray, followed by a left hook to the head. Then, as if in a kid's game of "now it's my turn," Robby came back with a right and two right uppercuts, again hurting Basilio. At the bell the 35,000 fans at Yankee Stadium were in bedlam, their voices as one, all cheering the two men who were putting on one of the greatest give-and-give battles in the history of boxing.

Robinson continued his assault in Round 14, but no man—let alone a 37-year-old wonder—could maintain the pace. Although his left jab continued to work, his motions were slower, wearier, more those of a 37-year-old. He hurt Basilio again, but couldn't follow it up. By the last round, he was circling and jabbing, experiencing trouble moving as Basilio dictated the pace. Then came the bell, and the fight was over.

When the unassailable sums and straight-angled figures on the three officials' scorecards were tabulated—the referee calling it 9–6, Robinson, and the two judges, 9–5–1 and 8–6–1, Basilio—Carmen Basilio was the new middleweight champion and Ray Robinson, for the fourth time, wore the title ex-middleweight champion of the world.

Afterward, each man, a winner in his own right, was to lose something. Basilio, the new middleweight king, automatically lost his welterweight crown, unable, by New York State law, to hold both crowns simultaneously. And Robinson lost his $500,000 purse, the IRS attaching it on "anticipated" income.

And yet whatever had happened, it couldn't be said, even by the heartiest of Robinson fans, that their man hadn't given his all. It was just that it wasn't the young Robinson whom Carmen had treated so indelicately. And therein lies the story of the fight, a great fight between two great fighters.

Archie Moore vs. Yvon Durelle
The Forum, Montreal, Canada
December 10, 1958

Throughout the ages, old men have been lionized in everything from literature (*The Old Man and the Sea*), to nursery rhymes ("Old King Cole") and song ("Ol' Man River"). But none of them held a candle to the old lion of the ring, Archibald Lee Wright, better known as Archie Moore.

There was only one Archie Moore. He was glib, elegant, quick of wit and of hands, the possessor of more knockouts than any man in history, and holder of a world's championship for a longer period of time than any other champion except two. But the Methuselah of the ring will be remembered not for any of those achievements, but instead for his performance on the night of December 10, 1958—the night he battled Yvon Durelle and proved that you can't keep a good man—young or old—down.

The road to that memorable night was paved with detours and plenty of hard rocks. Born in either Collinsville, Illinois, or Benoit, Mississippi, on either December 13, 1913, or December 13, 1916 (depending upon who was keeping score, Moore or his mother), Archie was either 42 or 45 years old the night of the fight. When asked about this discrepancy in his birthdate, the quick-thinking champion side-stepped and countered, "I have given this a lot of thought, and have decided that I must have been three when I was born."

Moore's first bout was in 1935 against Piano Mover Jones at Hot Springs, Arkansas. It ended in a second-round knockout for Moore, his first of a record-setting 141. It also began his long career in "bootleg" fights and tanktowns on the so-called Chitlin' Circuit, which was open to "colored" fighters who couldn't break into the big time. By 1936, Moore hit the highways and byways of backwater America, fighting some twenty-one times, mostly in and around his adopted hometown of St. Louis. He won eighteen fights, sixteen by KO, and was ready to make the bridge to the next rung on the fistic ladder, the small town clubs.

However, there were so many gradations to boxing back in the thirties that one boxer once asked his manager when he was booked for a fight in a town he had only a nodding acquaintance with, "Which one is it, small time, medium small-time, big small-time, little big-time, medium big-time, or The Bigtime?" And before Moore could even approach The Bigtime he had to pay his dues in more cities than anyone aside from Messrs. Rand and McNally ever heard of: cities like Keokuk, Quincy, and all points east, west, and south.

Moore fought twelve times in 1936 and won all twelve, ten by knockout, and the middleweight championships of Kansas, Oklahoma, and Missouri in the process. Now, it was on to the bigger time, if not The Bigtime, and Moore set sail for more lucrative boxing pastures in California, where he hoped to meet, and beat, the prominent middleweights fighting on the Coast and establish his credentials. However, as Moore's luck would have it, the day he arrived in San Diego was the day the boxing arena burned down.

This was the beginning of an unlucky streak that ran through Moore's early years: a severed tendon in the wrist here, a perforated ulcer that necessitated an operation to save his life there. If Moore had any luck, one wag suggested, it would have been "all bad."

But Moore, who was to survive more hardships than Job ever endured (including acute appendicitis, organic heart disorder, etc., etc., etc.), clung to his dual dreams that he would somehow come back and some day become a world champion.

Through dedication and perseverance he accomplished his first goal, coming back in 1942 to win his first five fights by KO. His second goal, however, took longer, much longer. It took him more than eleven years and fifty-eight knockouts to get a shot at a title.

Finally, on December 17, 1952, in front of his hometown fans, Archie Moore achieved his second goal, beating Joey Maxim decisively for the light heavyweight championship of the world. But even then Moore got the fuzzy end of the lollipop, earning only $800 for climbing to the pinnacle of his profession.

By now Moore's rocket had flown too close to the moon for him to be content with mere hang-gliding. He sought something more. He had to have something more than the $800 he received for winning a world's title. And, in the strange and wondrous way boxing operates, he got it. For along with Maxim's championship belt came Maxim's manager, the wily old Doc Kearns, the man who had guided Maxim—and, before him, Jack Dempsey and Mickey Walker—to the title.

It would be what Humphrey Bogart told Claude Rains at the conclusion of the film *Casablanca*, "the beginning of a beautiful friendship." Together they would forge a new trail on the fistic horizon, stepping over prone bodies on their way to the top. Over the next six years Moore would go to the post forty-three times, taking on all comers regardless of weight class, and dispatching twenty-five of them in fewer than the requisite number of rounds. His victims began whizzing by with all the rapidity of signs on the San Diego freeway, with names almost as recognizable: Bob Baker, Joey Maxim, Harold Johnson, Bobo Olson, Nino Valdes, James J. Parker, Eddie Cotton, Willie Besmanoff, Charlie Norkus, and Howard King, among others too plentiful to enumerate.

Only twice during these six years was he to come up short. Both times in heavyweight championship fights. The first time he lost to Rocky Marciano in nine rounds after knocking down the Rock in the second with a short right uppercut. The second time he lost to Floyd Patterson in a fight for Marciano's vacated throne. It was a fight that has never been fully understood.

Beaten, but hardly vanquished, Moore returned to the more comfortable environs of the light heavyweight division, defending his title about once a year. In 1957 he fought Tony Anthony, and in 1958 he fought Yvon Durelle. Therein lies the story of Moore's greatest fight.

Yvon Durelle was a mightily muscled fisherman out of the Maritime provinces of Canada. The third-ranked light heavyweight, he had brawled his way through 96 fights in 11 years, hammering out thirty-eight of his opponents and outstaying another thirty-six. Despite his record, which included six losses—all by KO—Durelle was thought to have two chances, little and none, of becoming the Canadian to win a world's title since Jackie Callura had captured the NBA featherweight title some fifteen years before. Many of the writers—and the betting gentry who had installed Moore as a 3–1 favorite—thought the fight a mismatch. In fact, the local correspondent from the *Montreal Gazette* thought so little of Durelle's chances that he wrote, "People snicker when the name of Yvon Durelle is placed alongside that of Archie Moore."

When Moore arrived at the prefight physical resplendent in a midnight-blue tuxedo, a black homburg, and waving a silver-topped walking stick, he looked like he was snickering, too, if not laughing outright as he paraded around in what he called his "morning clothes." But the last laugh that night was almost on ol' Archie.

For that night, at the Montreal Forum, Archie had hardly had time to take off his gaudy red velvet dressing gown with the silver trimmings and show off his trim 173½-pound waistline before the "fit hit the shan." Working inside, Durelle delivered a right hand over the top to Moore's head. Moore dropped to the canvas as if he had been hit with a sledgehammer, which he might have been. The referee, former heavyweight champion Jack Sharkey, started tolling over the inert form of what appeared to be the soon-to-be-former light heavyweight champion of the world.

After what seemed like an eternity—to Moore as well as to the 8,484 fans—the lifeless form beneath Sharkey stirred and righted itself on shaky legs at the count of nine. Durelle fairly flew from a neutral corner, cuffing the champion, and then, with another right, dropping him again. This time Moore was up without a count. Trying to hold on, to use every ounce of guile and mastery mustered in his twenty-four-plus years in the ring, Moore attempted to weather the storm created by the fisherman in front of him. He hid behind his gloves, raised armadillo fashion, throwing out an occasional left. But Durelle was all over him, attempting to end the fight early.

As the seconds ticked off, and the sand in Moore's eternal hourglass began to slip away, Durelle caught Moore with yet another right to the head, dropping him for the third time. Moore looked up at Sharkey as he tolled off the count, thinking, as he was to recall later, "Can this be me? Is this really happening to me?" (Later, much later, on the banquet circuit, he was to "remember" thinking to himself, "This is no place to be resting. I'd better get up and get with it.") And get up he did, at the count of nine, and somehow, someway, got through that first round, his longest round, fighting largely on instinct.

He was also able to take advantage of a mental lapse on the part of the challenger who later admitted that he didn't go for a knockout after the third knockdown because, "I forgot that this was a championship fight and that three knockdowns didn't halt the fight."

Round 2 found a totally different Moore coming out to face his challenger. No longer was he snickering. He was in a battle for his boxing life. He started jabbing and hooking with his left, staying away from the lethal right hand in front of him. He not only managed to hold off the stronger challenger, he won the round on most of the unofficial cards at ringside. But Durelle came back in Round 3, once again applying pressure and once spinning Moore around and catching him with a left and right that had the champion covering up.

Round 4 found both men flurrying, with Moore landing by far the flashier combinations and taking the play away from the challenger. So furious was the pace that their flurries continued far past the bell ending the round, angering both combatants. The fifth was a replay of the first with Durelle catching Moore with a wild left hook, sending him sprawling for the fourth time.

Suddenly, out of the cloud that had enveloped him for the first fifteen minutes of the fight, Moore went on the attack, using his left as a battering ram, keeping it in the face of the challenger and trying to set up the one punch that would end it. Occasionally he would alter his attack, coming up with left hooks and combinations, as he did twice in the sixth when he staggered Durelle and bloodied his nose, and once in the seventh, when he floored the challenger for a count of three. But it was the left, and almost exclusively the left, that won Moore rounds six through nine. That and the fact that the 29-year-old challenger was running out of steam while the 42-going-on-45-year-old champion was coming on stronger.

Moore's systematic attack began to wear the challenger down, and he began to miss with wild punches as the obviously tired Moore reached back into his bag of tricks, if not into his memory, and staggered Durelle with a hard right.

It might have been at that exact moment that the momentum of the fight changed, when the fight went out of Durelle. Or, it might have been between rounds when Doc Kearns wouldn't let Moore sit down in his corner, but instructed him, instead, to wave to his wife in the audience, telling Moore his wife was seated in the opposite corner when, in fact, she was behind him. Durelle, seeing Moore wave, thought he has waving at him, scornfully.

In the tenth, the bell began to toll for Durelle's Cinderella story as Moore carried the attack to his tired challenger, hitting Durelle with everything he threw—hooks, uppercuts, overhand shots, and right-hand chops. Near the end of the round Durelle collapsed under the cumulative weight of the fusillade, looking as far gone as Moore had nine rounds earlier. But the bell rang at eight, saving Durelle for one more round.

The eleventh was merely an extension of the tenth as an exhausted Durelle staggered out of his corner and fell down without being hit. Up at the count of nine, he ran into a short right to the chin and went down. And out.

Archie Moore had come back from the dead. The old man had done it again, adding another name to his list of KO victims, number 127 to be exact, breaking Young Stribling's record.

Archie Moore had retained his crown as king of the light heavyweights and became in one night the all-time king of knockout artists. But he had done something else as well: he had seemingly found the secret of longevity.

Cassius Clay vs. Sonny Liston
Convention Hall, Miami Beach, Florida
February 25, 1964

No event in recent American history, with the single exception of the assassination of President John F. Kennedy, is more shrouded in myth and mystery than the dethroning of heavyweight king Sonny Liston by Cassius Clay in Miami Beach on February 25, 1964.

Charles "Sonny" Liston was a much-maligned and badly misunderstood man—one who devoted most of his adult life to a clumsy quest for respectability. Jose Torres, former light heavyweight champion of the world and noted author, remembers Liston as "one of the most intelligent athletes I have ever met. He was so smart it wasn't even funny." But most of the world knew him as an ignorant, mean-tempered bully. This sharp difference between the man and his image may have had a great deal to do with his strange behavior on the night that he surrendered boxing's biggest prize.

Sonny was born into the family of an Arkansas sharecropper, a brutal drunkard who reportedly fathered twenty-five children. After an argument with his father, Sonny left home at the age of 13 to live with an aunt in St. Louis. There he drifted into a life of juvenile delinquency. At 16 he was already fighting with the local constabulary—their clubs against his fists. It was no contest, even then. Eventually he tried his hand at armed robbery. He was caught and sentenced to three concurrent five-year terms in the Jefferson City state penitentiary, an extremely harsh punishment for a young first offender.

A Roman Catholic prison chaplain had the foresight to suggest to inmate Liston that he channel his appetite for violence into boxing. Sonny agreed and quickly blossomed into a crude, but awesome talent. The authorities were sufficiently impressed to grant him a parole to pursue a career in the ring. In 1953, he captured the Chicago Golden Gloves heavyweight championship. A few months later he turned pro.

Blinkie Palermo, one of the mob figures who then controlled professional boxing, took an early interest in Liston's ring career. It was a Svengali-Trilby relationship that was at once Sonny's making and undoing. With Palermo's help Liston was given every opportunity to climb up the heavyweight ladder. He began to peak in August 1958, with a first-round knockout of tough Wayne Bethea in Chicago. The fight lasted all of 69 seconds. Just long enough for Bethea to lose seven teeth.

Sonny's first win over a recognized contender came six months later in Miami Beach, where he annihilated huge Mike DeJohn, the hardest-punching white heavyweight around and a darling of "Friday Night Fight of the Week" fans, in six rounds.

During the next four years Sonny Liston marched through the heavyweight division like Sherman through Georgia, leaving few survivors. Cleveland Williams, a ferocious puncher in his own right, fell in three of the most brutal rounds ever fought by big men. Liston, seemingly immune to pain, absorbed a series of the Big Cat's best punches without flinching.

Four months later, in August 1959, Nino Valdes, a man who had beaten Ezzard Charles, was dispatched in three rounds. In March 1960, Williams and Liston clashed again in Houston. In another incredible match, it took Sonny only two rounds to finish the job. A month later Roy "Cut and Shoot" Harris, who had gone twelve rounds in a title fight with Floyd Patterson, failed to survive three minutes with Liston. A third-round knockout of talented stylist Zora Folley in July 1960, and a 12-round decision over Eddie Machen in September of that year, entrenched Liston firmly in the number-one contender's slot, where he would languish for two long years.

The heavyweight division had never seen another man quite like him, a giant compressed into a six-foot, one-inch frame. His fists, fifteen inches in circumference, were bigger than Carnera's or Willard's. He had an eighty-four-inch reach, sixteen inches longer than Marciano's. He strengthened the muscles in his seventeen-inch neck by standing on his head for hours at a time. It was as if some futuristic geneticist had bred him in a test tube for the single purpose of beating up other men. His left jab knocked men out. It was in a class with Joe Louis's. His left hook was a lethal weapon, comparable to Joe Frazier's. He could go to the body with the ferocity of a Dempsey and launch a man toward the roof with an uppercut as powerful as George Foreman's. His right cross was a bit awkward, but he eventually perfected it into a deadly club.

But for all of his raw power and size, Liston's most remarkable attribute was psychological rather than physical. He made a science of inspiring fear in the hearts and minds of his opponents, breaking their wills with a stony stare during the referee's instructions, and stuffing towels under his robe to make his enormous physique look even bigger and more intimidating. In short, he was the meanest "mother" on the block, and not only didn't he care who knew it, he wanted everyone to know it.

Liston's carefully crafted techniques of intimidation were never more effective than they were against Floyd Patterson on September 25, 1962 when Liston finally got his chance to fight for the heavyweight title.

Patterson's super-cautious manager Cus D'Amato had persuaded Floyd to stay clear of Liston for over two years, but pride and embarrassment finally got the better of the champion. Patterson was beaten before the first punch was thrown. He came to Comiskey Park in Chicago with a disguise hidden in a brown paper bag, all the better to slink out of the stadium unnoticed if—or rather when—Sonny beat him. The fight lasted all of two minutes and six seconds. On July 22, 1963, Patterson tried again. This time he survived four seconds longer. Both bouts could better be described as muggings than heavyweight title bouts.

The new heavyweight champion was perhaps the least-liked man to hold the title since Jack Johnson. Newspaper editorials cried out for boxing commissions to strip him of his crown. The NAACP made haste to put distance between Liston and the "respectable" portion of the Negro race. And even President Kennedy had called for Patterson to deny him the chance to fight for the title. The title that he had sought for so long, believing that it would magically make him as popular as his idol, Joe Louis, turned out to be an albatross. With few contenders left in the division he had decimated, even Liston's chance to cash in on his crown seemed to be, at best, illusory. At worst, nonexistent.

• • •

A desperate search for a fresh face who could create box-office interest in a fight with the seemingly unbeatable Liston turned up a 22-year-old youngster from Louisville, Kentucky named Cassius Marcellus Clay. Clay first gained national recognition in 1960 by winning a gold medal in the light heavyweight division at the Olympic games in Rome. He turned pro in October 1960, under the tutelage of Angelo Dundee, who already had guided three other fighters to world titles.

Clay's early career proceeded apace, as he ran off a string of seventeen victories—including fourteen knockouts—against carefully chosen opponents. His style was a composite of extreme unorthodoxies in and out of the ring. He carried his hands low, some said dangerously low, as he moved in wide circles around an opponent, stabbing out with a long, incredibly quick left jab, and delivering punches in dazzling bouquets of six, seven, and eight at a time. When a punch came at his head, he pulled back instead of slipping underneath it, or to the side as "the book" dictated.

Clay grabbed headlines for himself by stealing a page from a professional wrestler named Gorgeous George. He assumed an arrogant pose that insulted opponents and irritated the working press. To compound matters, beginning with his fight with Lamar Clark in April, 1961, he began predicting, in doggerel, the exact round in which he would knock his opponent out. Incredibly, he made good on his predictions seven times, even disposing of contenders Alejandro Lavorante and 49-year-old Archie Moore in the promised round.

By March 13, 1963 while Sonny Liston was training for his rematch with Patterson, Cassius Clay, the punching poet, was big box-office news. An all-time-record crowd piled into Madison Square Garden, hoping to see an inflated light heavyweight named Doug Jones short-circuit Clay's prediction of a fourth-round knockout. And his career as well. They got more than they bargained for, as Jones, a notorious failure as a heavyweight, fought Cassius to a virtual standoff for ten rounds, only to lose a highly controversial decision.

Three months later Clay traveled to London to fight Henry Cooper, who was, like Jones, a fringe contender. Cooper possessed a heavy left hook and facial tissue as brittle as a 50-year-old coat of paint, tissue that gushed like a geyser when it broke under the impact of a punch.

Late in the fourth round "Our 'Enery" unloaded an exquisite short left hook which exploded against Clay's chin and knocked him on the seat of his pants along the ropes. Cassius wobbled to his feet just as the bell sounded and before Cooper could follow up his momentary advantage. Between rounds Angelo Dundee miraculously "discovered" a tear in Clay's glove, manufacturing an excuse for a new glove which delayed the beginning of Round 5 and saved Cassius from the inevitability of a knockout. He answered the bell for Round 5 and quickly turned Cooper's face into a real-life imitation of raw hamburger.

Even with his tarnished wins over Jones and Cooper, Clay found himself occupying the number-one contender's slot during a heavyweight talent drought. He was eager for a fight with champion Sonny Liston, but few observers gave him the chance of the proverbial snowball in hell. Some gave him even less.

Liston's best punch was a left hook—the same blow that had twice sailed over Clay's low guard and knocked him to the canvas, once by Cooper and once by Sonny Banks.

Clay's chance at the title was the successful culmination of a two-year campaign to get Liston into the ring, a campaign that began moments after Sonny's enormous arm was raised by the referee on the night that he was crowned champion. That night

Clay muscled his way through the crush in the ring at Comiskey Park where he stood face to face with Liston and issued a loud challenge. And when Liston set up camp for his rematch with Floyd in Las Vegas, Clay was right there, needling him incessantly during his workouts.

Sonny's training sessions were calculated to inspire fear. He could break a heavy bag with one punch. He juggled a medicine ball as if it was a peanut, to the sultry tune of his favorite song, "Night Train." But Clay wasn't impressed. He taunted Liston in the gyms and haunted Liston in the casinos, issuing insulting challenge after insulting challenge.

By November 1963, Liston had had enough. He agreed to fight Clay in Miami Beach the following February.

The Sonny Liston who signed to fight Clay admitted to being almost 32 years of age, but no official record of his birth existed. Friends placed his age closer to 40. Dating back to his close 12-round decision over Eddie Machen in September 1960, Liston had engaged in four fights that lasted a total of only six rounds. The fine edge he had honed in his climb to the top had been dulled with ring rust. The one-sided nature of his two first-round knockouts of Patterson had disguised the fact that by the ordinary standards of the ring Sonny was ready to be taken by the right opponent.

In compiling a 32–1 record, with twenty-one knockouts, Liston had traveled ten rounds only three times and twelve rounds once. Virtually all his important wins were quick knockouts. Even at his peak, when he was fighting regularly, he had never had to demonstrate great stamina.

Clay, an avid student of fight films, was endlessly curious about the particular strengths and weaknesses of his opponents. Dundee, his trainer, was perhaps the foremost analyzer of styles in the business. Together, they identified the obvious flaw in Liston's arsenal. Machen, a quick scientific boxer, adept at slipping punches and using the whole ring, had managed to last twelve rounds against Liston at his best and come within a couple of points of beating him. The lone loss on Liston's record had been inflicted by a little-known journeyman named Marty Marshall, who subsequently lasted a full ten rounds in another fight with Liston. Marshall, a defense-minded clown out of the Willie Meehan school, had frustrated Liston where better fighters had failed because he employed lateral movement. If Cassius Clay had mastered anything, it was lateral movement. If he could keep away from Liston until Sonny had depleted what had to be a limited supply of energy anything might happen.

Clay was not content to rely on speed and strategy. He attacked Liston with a well-orchestrated psychological divertissement, coming to a rousing climax at the prefight weigh-in.

Weigh-ins are generally uneventful. Both fighters are usually anxious to get away from the press for a few final hours of rest and quiet contemplation of combat. With the moment of truth approaching for Clay, Sonny must have anticipated that he would confront a chastened challenger at the weigh-in, one who would be vulnerable to the usual Liston intimidation.

Clay and his entourage, including Drew "Bundini" Brown, photographer Howard Bingham, Gene Kilroy, Dr. Ferdie Pacheco, and Angelo Dundee, arrived first. They were wearing big cowboy hats and waving placards. Even Dundee, normally a conservative man, was wearing a hat. Clay and Brown, his court jester and resident witch doctor, were chanting like lunatics: "Float like a butterfly, sting like a bee! Rumble, young man, rumble!" The mob of reporters in the room pressed forward, trying to make some sense out of the nonsense.

Liston walked into a madhouse. At first he couldn't even get close enough to Clay to fix his cold stare on him. When the two fighters were finally face to face, with the international media crowding around them to record the scene, Clay actually taunted Sonny and Brown had to "restrain" him. When commission doctor Alex Robbins took the challenger's blood pressure it registered at 200/100—an alarmingly high reading.

A confused press rushed back to their typewriters, still trying to figure out exactly what had happened. Relying heavily on what turned out to be a case of self-induced high blood pressure, they reported that Clay was gripped by fear. The press might have been fooled, but Liston wasn't. He knew the look of fear on a fighter's face and this wasn't it. Madness, perhaps, but not fear. And if there was anything that vibrated Liston's strings, it was someone "acting crazy."

Like most confirmed practical jokes, Liston hated nothing worse than being made a fool. After the final travesty of the weigh-in, Sonny was determined to make Clay pay dearly for his fun, which was exactly what Cassius had hoped for.

• • •

That night, in front of a disappointing crowd of 8,297 fans rattling around Miami's spacious Convention Hall, a more composed Clay met Liston again. This time, face to face in the center of the ring for the prefight instructions, it became apparent to Liston, for the first time, that Clay was larger, much larger, than he was. This would be no confrontation between a Jack and a giant—like the Liston-Patterson fights. Clay, although outweighed by eight pounds, 218 to 210, and giving away four inches in reach, stood a full two inches taller than Liston. It was a psychological victory for Clay, Liston never having fought anyone taller.

Liston tried once more with his famous death-ray eyes. Six towels had been stuffed under his robe, so that he looked like a wall of terrycloth. Clay met his gaze squarely. As referee Barney Felix gave his instructions, Clay hissed, "Chump! Now I got you, chump!" The shock must have hit Sonny harder than any punch he ever absorbed in the ring.

Liston was a somewhat mechanical fighter—a George Foreman trying to imitate Joe Louis. He had learned how to jab and feint and vary his punches. He knew how to cut off a ring. But his basic technique never changed: two steps forward, step again, and jab. Hook off the jab or follow it with a right. Two steps forward and so on and so on. Clay had studied films of Sonny's fights, taking note of his ponderous, patterned footwork and the heavy jab that packed enough power to knock down a wall.

As the bell sounded Liston lurched out of his corner, an energized Frankenstein coming to life. He nearly ran at Clay to begin the first exchange, but as soon as Sonny started his jab, Cassius slid gracefully to his left, away from the punch. Clay almost seemed to be running as he circled around the champion at a speed unheard of in a heavyweight contest. Liston jabbed and jabbed again, missing Clay's head by wide margins. The challenger's hands were almost dangling at his sides, leaving his head exposed to all kinds of mayhem. But each time Liston reached for it, it was gone, faster than you could say Cassius Marcellus Clay. As Clay moved to his left, Sonny made the correct adjustment, trying to decapitate him with a right hook. The punch missed. Liston kept shuffling forward moving quickly enough for Sonny Liston, trying to maneuver Cassius into a corner, but not quickly enough to catch him. Clay didn't throw one punch in anger until the round was almost over. A left jab, like a switchblade knife pulled out from under a coat, snapped into Sonny's face. Clay stopped moving and unleashed a flurry of lefts and rights to the champion's face. Liston seemed frozen in time. By the time he woke up and surged forward, Clay was on his bicycle and the bell had sounded. Liston stomped back to his corner, snorting mad. By surviving the first round, Clay had already won an important psychological victory.

For all of his anger and anxiety, Liston still remembered what he had been taught by his trainer, Willie Reddish. After only one round of chasing Clay, he concluded that he would not be able to take him out early with a single left hook to the head. First he would have to slow him down by clubbing his body, a process that Sonny was able to accomplish against most fighters in one or two rounds.

As the bell sounded to begin Round 2, Liston charged out of his corner, throwing heavy punches with both hands. Quickly he forced Clay against the ropes, where he dug brutal blows to Clay's liver and kidneys before Cassius could wriggle out to ring center. Still moving, almost galloping, to his own left as Sonny came straight at him, Clay picked his openings with the care of a master craftsman. His jab never missed and he always followed up with a fast combination before gliding out of danger. Each time he was hit, Liston froze, unable to counter Clay's blows.

A tiny cut, barely perceptible, opened on the champion's left cheekbone, under his eye. It was the first time in thirty-four professional fights that Liston had shed even a drop of blood. Sonny retaliated with a long left that was like a 234 coming out of a basement window, catching Clay with a meaningful punch for the first time in the fight. The challenger recalls, "It rocked me back. But either he didn't realize how good I was hit, or he was already getting tired and he didn't press his chance." In fact, it would be many years before anyone would be able to tag Clay with two damaging blows to the head in quick succession, and his ability to absorb punishment to the body would become legendary.

Round 3 saw Liston still pressing forward, hacking away at air, and Clay revolving clockwise around him. Sonny was moving just a little bit slower now. Still he was able to jolt the challenger with punches to the body that appeared to be inconsequential, but were, in fact, painful. "After the fight Clay's ribs and flanks were one big angry red welt," remembers the challenger's physician, Ferdie Pacheco.

Midway through the third session, Clay inflicted the first real damage of the fight. He feinted with his left and then drove a right uppercut into Sonny's cheek. The punch landed like an ice pick, and the once-tiny wound gaped open, spurting blood. Liston pawed at the cut, not completely believing what was happening. At the end of the third round he walked back to his corner, a weary man. For the first time he sat down.

During training for the fight Liston had sustained a very minor injury to his left arm or shoulder—the kind of slight damage that athletes habitually ignore when there is a big payday at stake. Liston's handlers had prepared for a possible aggravation of this minor injury by including a solution of alcohol and oil of wintergreen in their corner kit. During the early rounds, Sonny unleashed dozens of full force punches at Clay's head that missed everything. Swinging at air is more fatiguing to the muscles than hitting a target. Inevitably Liston's sore shoulder began to ache under the strain. Between Rounds 3 and 4 Sonny's corner was a busy place, as they worked to close the deep cut under his left eye and massaged his left shoulder with liniment.

Round 4 was the least eventful of the fight. Clay allowed Liston to work inside, sometimes covering up instead of moving laterally. The challenger, who had gone ten rounds only three times, was pacing himself for a 15-round bout. And, as Cassius walked back to his corner at the end of the round, he was squinting and blinking. A bit of Liston's liniment had gotten into Clay's eye. As Dundee wiped the fighter's face with a sponge, more of the fiery substance went into both of his eyes, leaving him momentarily blind. He was frightened. No man, however brave, would willingly take on a wounded beast like Liston without full sight. In the challenger's corner they were unaware that the liniment had caused the problem. Clay wondered if Dundee hadn't put something in his sponge. He looked to Drew Brown, holding up his gloves, and screamed, "Cut them off!" Referee Barney Felix came over to see what the confusion was about. Dundee, halfway down the steps leading out of the ring, came back up, pushed Clay out into the ring with one hand, and snatched the stool out from under him with the other. "This is the big one, daddy!" he shouted as he launched his fighter into action.

All of this had not gone unnoticed in the champion's corner. Indeed, in two of his previous fights, Liston's opponents had complained about their eyes "burning." Liston now looked at Clay "like a kid looks at a new bike on Christmas," remembers Ferdie Pacheco. He came at Cassius with renewed energy, swinging his big fists like a pair of meat cleavers. How clearly Clay could see is still not certain. He walked out on unsteady legs, holding out his left hand like a blind man's cane. Sonny quickly backed him against the ropes. Clay leaned back, pushing his left glove into Sonny's face, slipping those punches he could see. Referee Barney Felix thought seriously about stopping the fight.

At first Liston's punches got through—agonizing wallops to the midsection and a couple of left hooks to the head. Clay began to move blindly around the ring on instinct as his corner tried to guide him and Liston tried to tear his head off. Then his eyes began to clear just as Sonny was slowing down and not throwing so many punches—and missing most of them. As the round drew to a close, Clay began lashing out with needle-sharp jabs, raising red welts under both of Liston's eyes.

Referee Barney Felix had the ring doctor take a precautionary look at Clay's eyes between Rounds 5 and 6. On the other side of the ring, Liston's corner was a somber place. The champion was clearly tired now, having already boxed just one round less than he had fought in the preceding three-and-a-half years.

Like a man trudging off to the guillotine knowing what fate had in store for him, Sonny Liston shuffled out in the sixth round to face the fastest and perhaps the greatest heavyweight fighter in history. Quickly Clay went on the attack, missing with a left hook, but scoring with a wicked right-left combination to the head. When Liston failed to return the fire, Clay machine-gunned him with six consecutive unanswered punches—three lefts, followed by three rights. Sonny jabbed back listlessly and Clay ripped home a pair of lefts into the soon-to-be ex-champion's lumpy face. Clay then moved out to long range, circling and jabbing with surgical precision. The punches made a loud, painful thud as they wacked into Liston's sad face. There was a purple lump under the champion's right eye and a four-inch gash under his left one. Cassius missed with a big right that drew a rise from the crowd. He drilled holes in Sonny's head with his left, driving it into his face four times in succession. Sonny responded with a solid, short right that was his last hurrah, but Clay made him pay for his folly with two more razor-sharp lefts. The crowd roared its approval at the bell.

As Clay went back to his stool he shouted at the press section, "I'm gonna upset the world!"

Both corners worked feverishly on their fighters for fifty seconds of the allotted minute between Rounds 6 and 7. At the ten-second buzzer Clay was on his feet, glaring across the ring at Liston who was slumped on his stool, the sand slowly sifting out of his championship glass. Some observers claim that a tear coursed down his wounded cheek. Liston opened his mouth and spat his mouthpiece out onto the canvas, as if it had a bad taste. Suddenly, the fight was over. Liston's manager, Jack Nilon, had stopped it because of what he said was "the severe pain in Liston's left shoulder."

Clay, looking like his feet were afire, leapt around the ring. "King!" he bellowed. "Eat! Eat! Eat your words! I am the king! I am the king!" he shouted to the forty-six newspapermen at ringside, forty-three of whom had picked Liston.

It was anyone's guess what really went through the bruised, confused head of Sonny Liston as he sat on his stool between the sixth and seventh rounds. His was a head that had been hit with policeman's clubs and filled with the strange paranoia of the underworld. Being the champion couldn't have been much fun for Sonny, not with the leaders of his own race, the press, and even the President of the United States lined up against him, and God knows what kind of creatures crawling out of his shady past to claim repayment for old favors.

You sensed that when Sonny Liston spat out his mouthpiece, he was spitting out the rotten, bitter fruits of a success that was really just one more disguised failure in the life of this unlucky man.

Muhammad Ali vs. Joe Frazier
Madison Square Garden, New York
March 8, 1971

Just as the making of a great martini must be the correct mating of gin and vermouth at precisely the right moment, not a second too early nor one too late, so too is the making of a great fight, one made at precisely the right moment.

Such was the case with the Muhammad Ali and Joe Frazier on that night of March 8, 1971, a fight which possessed all the right ingredients of a great fight: two undefeated heavyweight champions, fighting for the most money ever earned by an athlete, let alone a boxer, fought in the midst of a turbulent debate over the Vietnam conflict with one of the participants adopted by those in support of the war, the other by those opposed, and held in the mecca of boxing, Madison Square Garden, in front of a riotous assemblage.

It was a fight that captured the imagination not just of the fight fans, but of the entire world. It was not merely another of the "Fights of the Century," which, according to the boxing historians, had already totaled up to centuries far beyond Flash Gordon's twenty-fifth, but, as boxing scribe Barney Nagler dubbed it, "The Fight."

The weeks leading up to the fight had writers everywhere reducing their pencils down to stubs covering it like the Creation of the World, part II, chronicling everything and anything about it and its participants. Ali's prefight doggerel had him saying, "They call Joe Frazier 'Smokin' Joe' because he talks about he's hot. He always talks about he's gonna come out smokin'. So I wrote a poem and it describes what happens:

Joe's gonna come out smokin'.
And I ain't gonna be jokin'.
I'll be pecking and a-pokin'
Pouring water on his smokin'.
This might shock and amaze ya,
But I'm gonna re-tire Joe Frazier.

On the other glove, Joe Frazier made no such request upon the art of conversation, instead saying only: "He calls me 'Uncle Tom' and I call him a phony." No match for Ali in their prefight hoopla, Frazier had hung up the phone on Ali during a commercial being filmed for the hair tonic Vitalis, not wanting to put up with Ali's "jive." He would save his talking for the ring.

The scene that Monday night in '71 would have done justice to the worst excesses of the French Revolution. Hours before the doors officially opened at 7:30, thousands, both with and without tickets, milled around outside Madison Square Garden, there to be seen and obscene. Amongst the crowd could be seen scalpers offering one-hundred-and-fifty dollar tickets for seven hundred a pop, men preening and prancing around in full-length white mink coats and women in extreme clothes, sporting everything from twelve-inch-down-the-knee slit skirts to low-cut blouses and five-inch heels. And everywhere more fur than could be found on an Alaskan range.

When the doors to the Garden finally opened, many went through hell just to make their entrance. Even those with tickets had to wait an hour as the crowd surged toward the doors. One woman, in tears, had just given her ticket to a ticket-taker when a mysterious hand materialized out of nowhere to snatch it from her. The doorman, a witness to what happened, was powerless to redress her loss.

As the 17,000-plus filled the cavernous arena, there, at ringside, could be seen the celebrities du jour: the notables, quotables, and even those who weren't household names in their own households, all of whom created a stir once identified. At ringside could be seen Burt Lancaster, doing the commentary for the closed-circuit audience; LeRoy Neiman, sketching the goingson; and the photographer for *Life Magazine,* Frank Sinatra. And up in the balcony, (the balcony for Chrissakes!) was former vice president, Hubert Humphrey.

Finally, after what seemed an eternity, the house lights go down and the people rise to their feet in one noisy mass. For there he is, emerging from the shadows, clad in red robe and red tasseled shoes, throwing punches in the air as he dances down the aisle: Muhammad Ali. Commotion! Chaos!

As he steps into the ring, he extends his arms in the air, and the crowd, now his congregation, let out with a two-syllabic chant: "Al-li, Al-li, Al-li!" He rewards them with his famous "Ali Shuffle" and the crowd goes wild.

Then, almost as if a choirmaster had waved off the noise, the crowd begins to settle back in their seats only to rise again as another familiar figure comes down the aisle: Joe Frazier. His entrance is more subdued, his pace more measured, as Frazier, berobed in a velvet-brocaded outfit, green and gold, shuffles toward the ring, throwing punches, his eyes straight down, all business. The crowd, recognizing him, lets out with another cheer, almost equal to the one given Ali just seconds before.

Now the two fighters are in the ring, attended by their entourage—Ali by Angelo Dundee and "Bundini" Brown and Frazier by Yank Durham—as ring announcer Johnny Addie reaches for the microphone coming down from the ceiling. The crowd hushes, bursting into wild applause only when the fighters' names are announced. Referee Arthur Mercante then brings the two fighters to the center of the ring for their last-minute instructions and they return to their respective corners to hear last-second advice and exhortations from their handlers.

And then, the bell! Frazier walks straight in, Ali comes in a circle, both meeting almost in the center of the ring. Ali feints with a left, Frazier walks in, missing his own jab. Frazier misses with another jab and Ali counters with one of his own. Frazier keeps coming, a one-dimensional machine, his body weaving, his hands moving up and down, his chin buried in his chest, pursuing Ali. Ali stops and throws a jab. Another jab. Many of his punches are missing and Frazier keeps coming. Ali stops again, throws a jab, steps back, feints, throws a fast jab and follows with a right cross, then an even faster left hook/right cross combination, many of the punches missing the crouching Frazier, who keeps boring in at the same pace. Frazier connects for the first time with a right to Ali's chest. Ali keeps moving. He moves straight back and Frazier follows. It is relentless pressure. They go inside now and Ali pushes Joe to the side and hits him with a jab. Ali smiles. Frazier throws a left that falls short again. The bell.

Round 2. Again Ali comes to the center of the ring in a circle. Again, he feints. Frazier jumps back and jumps back in, but is unable to reach the taller Ali. Ali stops and throws a barrage of punches. Now Ali moves with Frazier chasing him, maintaining the same exact pace. Ali's eyes seem transfixed on Frazier's forehead; Frazier's on Ali's chest. Ali circles Frazier, first to his right, then to his left, throwing jabs. Frazier is following him, not cutting off the ring, his pace turtle-like compared to Ali's. Frazier connects with a jab to Ali's head. Another falls short as Ali comes back with one of his own that misses. The bell ends Round 2.

Ali stands in his corner, his mouthpiece still in place, listening to Dundee—and occasionally to Bundini, who remains quiet when Dundee talks—while, over in the other corner, Frazier listens to the calm, soothing tones of Durham, who alternately wipes down his face and doles out advice. The bell for Round 3. Frazier starts out of his corner per normal invoice, walking straight to Ali. But this time Ali doesn't circle, but instead meets Frazier in his corner, then retreats two, three steps back into the ropes. Frazier begins to work Ali over. A wild left by Frazier. Ali pulls back his head at the last second and the air generated by the blow air conditions the first two rows. Ali remains on the ropes and Frazier continues to look for openings, connecting with a right to the body and then launching another long, left hook, which misses its mark again.

Ali is still on the ropes and Frazier hits him with a vicious left. A right hits Ali's face as it moves away. A fast hook grazes Ali on the right side of his face. Ali tries to move, but Frazier won't let him. Joe pushes Ali back to the ropes. Ali smiles. Now Frazier smiles. Another hook by Frazier lands on Ali's face, but Ali sees it coming and rolls with the punch. Ali gets off the ropes, Frazier pursuing, coming forward, like a tank. Frazier throws some vicious punches, but Ali shakes his head "No," signifying to the crowd that he is not hurt. His fans laugh and cheer. Ali now smiles at the crowd. Again, his crowd laughs and applauds. Meanwhile, Joe is punching furiously: a left hook, a right, another hook. Frazier is making the fight. Ali retaliates with a flurry, almost pitty-pat punches. Now Frazier is the one who laughs. The "other crowd" laughs with him. A mean left hook that Ali never saw just misses and the round ends where it began: with Ali on the ropes.

There had been a change in the momentum of the fight. The transition was being forced on Ali by Frazier, with Frazier pinning Ali on the ropes and banging away with murderous punches while Ali, on occasion, responded with combinations, catching the oncoming Frazier. But Ali's responses were just that: occasional, not often. For Ali, he may well have experienced the worst round of the 204 he had fought in his pro career.

The fourth and fifth rounds would be more of the same. If you were writing footnotes, you could write ibid.

Ali has now begun sitting on his stool between rounds. His breathing is heavy, but no more so than Frazier's in the opposite corner, both fighters working under tremendous pressure.

In the sixth, Ali seems to move more. Jabs and moves. Jabs again. Frazier hasn't changed, he's still coming in. Ali begins throwing uppercuts at a head that doesn't stop moving. Ali retreats to the ropes and jabs at Frazier, who doesn't look like he has the same drive. The momentum swings again. Ditto, round seven.

In the eighth, two seemingly tired fighters face off against each other. Ali again goes to the ropes and Frazier tees off, missing his target with seven punches. Ali drops his hands, daring Joe to hit him. Frazier, too, drops his, and Ali accommodates him, throwing a one-two combination that hits Frazier flush on the face, above the jaw. Now Frazier is the one laughing. Frazier's tree trunk-like legs push him toward Ali and Ali goes back to his favorite spot: the ropes. Frazier lashes out with another of his attacks. The round ends.

Ali is welcomed back to his corner by two open mouths. They are telling him off. He's fooling around. And fooling himself as well. For every time Ali invites Joe to come and punch, Joe accommodates him, Ali doing nothing in return. And, in doing so, Frazier is showing both the confidence and the will to win.

Round 9 has Ali moving beautifully again, looking like he has found his "second wind" and snapping his jab off in Frazier's face.

When Ali moves and punches he makes the slow-moving Frazier seem amateurish and slow. It's now that kind of fight for Ali.

But, in Round 10, Ali reverts to the Ali of old, the Ali of Rounds 3, 4 and 5, retreating to the ropes where Joe begins his work again. He is throwing fewer punches than before, but making more contact. A wicked left hook lands to Ali's body. A right to Ali's forehead. Ali seems to be resting, Frazier chasing. Frazier missed a lot, especially with wicked left hooks, but he was doing something; Ali, nothing. Then, in the last twenty seconds of the round, Ali tried to steal it, throwing one . . . two . . . three jabs. All direct hits. Then a left/right combination of his own. The bell. The fight is two-thirds over and Ali is seemingly in command of his own destiny with the "championship rounds," Rounds 11 through 15, to go.

But then comes Round 11. And everything changes again. For as Ali goes back to his favorite resting spot, like a tiger remembering its favorite place, Frazier is on him. And then a left hook from hell catches Ali on the button. His legs shake, he can't control them. Frazier goes on the attack. He rakes Ali's body with vicious punches. A right to the body, a left to the body, now Frazier pushes Ali back against the ropes. Another sinful left hook! Ali's legs, strangers to each other, buckle. His eyes are glassy. He looks like he's going to the canvas. In his entire career he has never been hurt this badly. Ali's will struggles to keep him on his protesting legs. Frazier is punching, his muscles forcing his arms to move faster, stronger. Ali begins playing games, pretending he is hurt worse than he really is, momentarily halting Frazier's forward movement as he considers whether his opponent is playing possum. Then it's back to the attack. Finally, the bell ends the one-sided round.

Bundini is up on the apron of the ring, throwing water at Ali who walks slowly to his corner. Water splashes some of the newsmen at ringside. Ali slumps on the stool. Dundee works on his weak legs. Bundini pours water over Ali's head and back.

Round 12 finds Ali moving slowly out of his corner, using his damaged legs, trying to overcome the beating he got in the previous round. He moves to his right, now to his left. Frazier resumes his attack, pinning Ali against the ropes once again. Ali keeps his right hand close to his cheek, all the better to avoid those savage hooks to his chin. The round plays itself out with Ali trying to recover from the horrific beating he took in Round 11.

The thirteenth begins like all the previous three rounds: Ali, with back to the ropes, Frazier, applying more pressure than an army of acupuncturists, on the attack. Frazier now looks like a man who has been pushing a loaded truck uphill for thirty-six looooong minutes, but shows no signs of stopping short of his goal as long as his energy holds out. For three more minutes he's everlastingly at it, backing Ali up, beating on him, dealing out more punishment. And Ali's taking it. The noise at the end of the round tells it all with Frazier's crowd, some of them having backed their man with money at the 7–5 odds he commanded as the favorite, aroar, and Ali's constituency murmuring with concern.

The bell for the fourteenth quiets the crowd. A little. Ali is again pulled by the magnetism of the ropes. Frazier swings twice with wild lefts. And misses. Now, somehow, someway, Ali escapes from his self-made prison of ropes to come out to the center of the ring and is the one doing the swinging. He connects with a vicious left hook to Frazier's head. A right. He pushes Joe back and hits him with a one-two combination. Ali looks like a new man, a revitalized man, as he explodes with punches to Frazier's head. Ali is now a moving target; a moving target leaving punches to be remembered by.

Could it be that Ali has once again changed the course of the fight? That he still has a chance to pull it out? That Frazier has punched himself out and that Ali has found new life? These were the questions going through everyone's mind as the bell sounded, ending Round 14.

Last round! Expectation is still the word to describe the excited crowd. No one is sure who is ahead. Some say Ali, some say Frazier. But nobody, nobody, is yelling one-sided now.

Both meet in the center of the ring for the ritualistic touching of the gloves, Frazier coming out of his corner in a determined gait, Ali a little more deliberately. Ali moves back, toward his corner, with Joe almost on top of him. Ali moves to his left. He now moves to the center of the ring. He moves straight back to the south side of the ring. He moves his left foot back, as if to throw a punch. Joe starts a left hook. He pulls it back and reloads, then leaps off the floor to launch it, getting all 205½ pounds behind it. Ali is moving his head back slowly, looking away from the punch. The left hook explodes on Ali's exposed jaw. For only the third time in his career Ali crashes to the canvas, his eyes glazed.

One second passes and Ali's eyes are trying to focus desperately. Mercante's count goes to "three" and Ali, by force of will, lifts himself off the mat, taking the mandatory eight-count. He walks toward Joe on unsteady feet, the right side of his face distorted from the power of Joe's malevolent left hook. The damage from that one blow is irreparable. Frazier has just won the fight. The impact of that one blow took everything Ali had left. He is there strictly to finish the fight on two feet. Moments later, Frazier, on the attack, jolts his 215-pound rival with another left hook. But Ali holds on. With a minute remaining in the round, and the fight, Ali tries to go for a knockout. But his punches have no effect on Frazier. With the crowd roaring, the bell rings and Frazier playfully cuffs Ali across his head, hung in acknowledged defeat.

The decision, read by Johnny Addie—Judge Bill Recht, eleven rounds to four, Frazier; Judge Artie Aidala, nine rounds to six, Frazier; and Referee Arthur Mercante, eight rounds to six, one even, Frazier—merely verified what everyone already knew: that Joe Frazier had won "The Fight."

But even though Frazier had won "The Fight," the people's hearts had been won by Ali. In subway after subway leading away from Madison Square Garden that chilly March night, signs could be seen etched in the artistic medium of the "little" people, spray paint reading: "Ali Lives."

George Foreman vs. Joe Frazier
Kingston, Jamaica
January 22, 1973

A funny thing happened to Joe Frazier on his way to a multi-million dollar return bout with Muhammad Ali: He met George Foreman in a match called "The Sundown Showdown." And, in a blowout as elementary as any since Jack Dempsey had annihilated Jess Willard some half-century earlier, the young challenger dissembled "Smokin' Joe" in just 275 seconds.

With shoulders like those of a blacksmith and arms like battering rams, Big George was unbeaten in thirty-seven fights, thirty-four of those knockout wins. But common wisdom asked, "Who'd he ever beat?" and installed him as a 3–1 underdog to the supposedly "invincible" Frazier, winner of all his twenty-six fights and conqueror of Muhammad Ali. Still, Foreman thought he could do it, and that was all it was to take.

At the opening bell, "Smokin' Joe" came out in his patented bob and weave. Pressing the attack, he set up shop in mid-ring, all the better to work his way under the seventy-eight-and-one-half inches-reach of the challenger and throw his potent left hook. But Foreman met him head-on, never taking a backward step, and started probing at the champion's head with a left.

One of those in Foreman's corner, Doc Broadus, had scouted Frazier during his training sessions to look for secret moves. He told Foreman, "I didn't see any. He just led with his head, same as always. George, drop that hammer on him." And that's just what George did, frescoing him with a thunderous right to the head as Frazier waded in, head up and unprotected.

Falling base over apex, Frazier's seat had barely touched the canvas before he jumped up and once again tried to work his way back inside. But after an exchange of punches, Foreman unloaded with a series of rights to Frazier's head. Once again, Frazier went to the canvas. Wearing the look of a man who had eternally been put upon, a dazed Frazier arose quickly. But just as quickly, he was deposited back on the canvas by a howitzer shot of a right that Foreman delivered just as the bell sounded to end the first round.

Frazier rushed out for the second round, trying mightily to land his left hook. But Foreman picked off the punches, and in return, landed a woodchopping right and left to the champion's jaw, sending Frazier to the mat for the fourth time. Frazier, with powers barely those of respiration and locomotion, got up only to be knocked down yet again. Frazier struggled to his feet once again, where this time, he ran into a series of punches, punctuated by a pluperfect right uppercut. The punch lifted the fireplug form of Frazier straight up in the air, defying gravity, like a tree stump pulled out of the ground.

And still he tried to regain his feet. As he stood there, unsure of what was going on—or going wrong—referee Arthur Mercante Sr. signaled the end of Frazier's reign at 1:35 seconds of the second round and six knockdowns. Now, to those who asked, "Who'd he ever beat?", George Foreman could answer "Smokin' Joe" Frazier. Badly.

Aaron Pryor vs. Alexis Arguello
The Orange Bowl, Miami, Florida
November 12, 1982

Belief is a funny word. It's made up of one part hope, one part perception, and one part realization—with a sprig or two of bias thrown in for good measure. And boxing has more than its share of beliefs-cum-biases, especially where great matches such as the Pryor–Arguello match are concerned.

When the fight itself was announced you had to believe that this would be one helluva match-up: The unflappable, almost unbeatable Alexis Arguello going for his fourth title—something even the immortal Henry Armstrong could not bring off—versus the undisciplined style of Aaron Pryor, a Waterpik out of control, running amok in the trappings of a boxer. The match-up was so good, in fact, that writers converging on Miami before the fight had already ceded it "Fight of the Year" honors before the first punch was thrown in anger.

Belief dictated that Arguello would be the matador, Pryor the bull, with Arguello, one of the fiercest body punchers in the history of the sport—so fierce, in fact, that when he hit Cornelius Boza-Edwards a shot to the labonza, Boza-Edwards lost control of his bodily functions and actually soiled his trunks—implanting his bondaleros into the unprotected gut of Pryor until the final kill. Unless, of course, Pryor was to get to him early. The beliefs, and the theories, went on and on. Pryor early, Arguello late went one. Pryor was easy to hit, even knock down, especially if KO Kameda could knock him head-over-belt, went another. Legs, went still another, tend to rebel against an older fighter's wishes and in the later rounds have a mind of their own. And, the ropebirds suggested, champions from lower divisions fail more often than not in their upwardly-mobile challenges across the divisional Rubicon. Finally, there were many from the good-little-man-good-big-man school who held that punchers cannot take their power with them when they transcend a division's boundaries, the weight displacement working against them geometrically rather than arithmetically.

But, for forty minutes and six seconds, belief was in a constant state of suspension, as first one and then another of the preconceived beliefs were knocked into someone or other's cocked hat.

The evening at Miami's Orange Bowl had started in a strange manner, destroying any belief anyone put into local boxing commissions. Starting with the absence of a bell (because, as one commissioner put it, "The man who had the bell was a timekeeper who was not assigned to the main event and I guess he told everybody to 'go to hell' and took off,") down through the lack of stools for fighters, the Miami commissioners paid an amazing lack of attention to details. With six inspectors assigned to cover the two dressing rooms, five fewer than the number assigned showed up, meaning that one of the two dressing rooms would always be uncovered. With the psyche running about as rampant as the flu on a cold winter's night, this oversight allowed those in the Pryor camp to try to throw a prefight intimidation into Arguello, much as they were trying to pump up their own man, screaming in unison, "It's Hawk Time" in response to their own exhortation, "What time is it?" But the inspector's absence almost took on tragic overtones in light of the prefight hysteria surrounding the presence of Nicaraguan Sandinista forces in the audience who would try to "get" at expatriate Arguello. (In fact, one man with a gun was apprehended near the Arguello dressing room, with the three-time champ hurried into the shower.)

Despite the boxer commissioners acting like anything but, the two fighters somehow made it into the ring, fighting their way through the crowd at ringside and even through their own hangers-on, now filling every corner of the ring, proving that nature and prefight championship fights both abhor vacuums. In fact, it was a similar prefight mob scene before the Pryor-Kameda fight that caused the predestined loser, KO Kameda, to complain, "I had no room to warm up, that's why I lose fight."

Now the two warriors stood still, at least momentarily, Pryor frozen with his newly-wrapped hands extended in his menacing hawk pose, Arguello transfixed, staring at the mob scene across the ring while doing a little hop, skip, and jump in place. Two national anthems later, the dim bell somewhere in the bowels of the Bowl rang and the long-awaited match was underway.

As predicted, Pryor came out blazing, throwing lefts and rights to the head, the shoulders and any other anatomical part of Arguello that might have been visible. Arguello, for his part, pawed back with a left hook, throwing it in the general direction of the hurricane hovering around his head. Then, after Pryor forced him to give ground, Arguello threw his first right of the fight, catching Pryor with a straight right. Suddenly Pryor staggered backwards. Momentarily. And came back firing. It was a pattern that would be repeated time and again, as he caught

Arguello with two punches that caused the three-time champ to lift his foot from the canvas, stung by the fury of the attack.

In Round 2, Pryor came out at Arguello in so many directions it looked like he had just taken a four-way cold tablet and decided he had three more ways to go to catch up to it. Lead rights, rights following rights, and left-rights, all the while changing his positioning and angles on Arguello. The latter was reaching out and beginning to find the now-he's-there-now-he's-not Junior Welterweight Champion with an occasional left and even two rights, which landed flush and would have, under normal conditions, started an avalanche. Only they didn't. Pryor took them and, after brushing them off as one would a pesky mosquito, went back on the attack.

Round 3 found Arguello beginning to land his vaunted one-two, a left to the body and a right to the head, once forcefully enough to drive Pryor's head and torso out between the ring ropes. After referee Stanley Christodoulou had saved him, Aaron went back to work. Only this time he added something new to his already fully stocked arsenal, a left jab and a right uppercut. Still, Arguello caught him in a toe-to-toe slugging match off the ropes and won his first round.

By the fourth, Aaron's punches-in-bunches had produced a long, angular cut alongside Alexis's eye and once again established his control of the fight; again despite getting caught with a punch that later Arguello's personal manager Bill Miller would describe as having the force to "fell King Kong." As the rounds continued at their breakneck pace, one had to begin wondering when either one of the following two scenarios would play out: (1) Pryor would wind down, like a toy whose spring has been wound too tight; or (2) The ageless legs of Arguello, which had carried him to seventy-six wins in eighty fights, would begin to show the inevitable erosion of pressure.

Throughout the middle rounds, Alexis continued to pursue Pryor, his one-two landing more frequently; but unfortunately for him, Aaron's center of balance, as unpredictable as the man possessing it, carried him out of harm's way every time. Arguello tried to press his advantage, reducing Aaron to a two-shot fighter. Pryor now admitted he was "worried" about the stretch drive, having heard so much about Alexis's killer ability in the final rounds. Indeed, when the fight came into Arguello's "turf," the lightweight champ began to take charge, driving the plucky junior welterweight champ back with one and two punches. But never more, his ability to follow up negated by the fact that Pryor's footwork took on the look of a Ray Bolger with St. Vitus.

In the thirteenth Arguello, now nicked both above and below the left eye, took a bead on his opponent and caught him repeatedly with his patented left to the body and right to the head. Exhorted by his corner to keep coming at him, "You're the champ," Pryor would come back in, usually with a lead right, only to find Arguello's own right placed against his nose. Twice Arguello caught Pryor with right hands that would have folded any other fighter within the next six weight divisions that night. But not Pryor. Maybe it was just that Aaron, who came back in with a vengeance every time he was hit, found that every clout had a silver lining. Or maybe it was that Arguello, at 138½, couldn't displace the 140-pound Pryor as he had so many lesser weights. Whatever, after thirteen the fight was even on Ring's card, 124–124, reflecting the closeness of the fight as seen by the three officials, two of whom had Pryor ahead by three and one judge Arguello ahead by two.

A funny thing happened on the way to the fourteenth round. In Aaron's corner, at least. For toward the end of the sixty-second break, and after breaking yet another spirit of ammonia capsule under Pryor's nose, his trainer, Panama Lewis, abruptly grabbed the water bottle handed him by cutman Artie Curley and demanded something that sounded like, "Give me the other one . . . the one I mixed . . ." and proceeded to give the second bottle to Aaron, who swallowed it rather than spit it out.

With the swig and snort under his belt, Aaron charged right back to the fray, landing a left and a right, another left and a left hook. Then, in the center of the ring and with Arguello trying to set up another of the one-two that had been taking their toll of Aaron for the last three rounds, Pryor put his punching machine into high gear and rattled off a volley of six punches, the last of which, straight right, caught Arguello flush, sending him straight back into the ropes and aging him instantly.

Pryor, known as a "finisher" par excellence, was on him in a trice, raking him with punch-after-punch as Arguello's mouth fell open, his black mouthpiece giving him the eerie look of a grotesque jack-o'-lantern as his head lolled on his neck and his eyes sought their sockets. Twenty-three punches, accentuated by three devastating rights coming one after another, prompted referee Christodoulou to jump in, his arms waving like the wings of a giant pelican, and signal the end of Arguello's dream.

As Alexis slumped to the canvas, his dreams behind him as well as ahead of him, the majority of the 23,800 fans in the Orange Bowl fell silent, their fears with him, their hopes shattered, their beliefs as crumbled as the form on the floor. When, after some four minutes, he finally stirred, they did too, feeling as he felt, now believing that Aaron Pryor was the better man.

Gone now were their second guesses, the questions about what was in the bottle. ("Peppermint schnapps" answered Artie Curley when he happened by the table of a *New York Times* columnist and yours truly after the fight. "He had a late meal and he was burping when hit in the stomach.") They knew, as all did, that the gods of chance were against Alexis in his try for a fourth championship. Aaron Pryor was the better man. And that was all they had to believe in the fight that was indeed "The Fight of the Year."

Roberto Duran vs. Sugar Ray Leonard I
Olympic Stadium, Montreal, Canada
June 20, 1980

Vince Lombardi, sport's premier winner, was so sure of his success that his strategy consisted of but one tactic: "I'll give the other team my game plan and plays. If they can stop them, they'll win; if they can't, I'll win."

Sugar Ray Leonard tried the exact same approach. Only this time, Roberto Duran stopped it. And won.

The difference between Lombardi and Leonard reduced itself to one distinction: Lombardi was talking about using his strength(s), not the other guy's. Challenging his opponent to make the mistakes, and taking advantage of him when he didn't respond correctly. Leonard, on the other hand, was determined to use his opponent's strength, not his own. Therein lay the underlying weakness in Sugar Ray's battle plan.

And so, he of the lightning fists and well-defined moves, inexplicably took on the man with the hands of stone and the straight-forward, but subtle, moves in a deadly game—a game of "Machismo." And, as he must, he lost. Not only because the word "Macho" is a Spanish word meaning "courage and aggressiveness"—today given new meaning by a Spanish-speaking

Panamanian, whose forebears had invented the word Duran was to perfect—but because he was destined to lose playing another man's game; a game which played into Duran's hands—"of Stone."

The battle plan against Duran was Sugar Ray's idea and his alone. "I surprised a lot of people with my tactics . . . ," he was to say after the fight. "I fought Duran a way I thought I could beat him." Angelo Dundee concurred, saying only that, "It was his plan. He had it in his head that he was stronger than Duran." Even before the man with the plan entered the ring, Roberto Duran had scored the first punch, psychologically. Entering the ring a full two minutes before the-then WBC welterweight champion, Duran had beamed to the crowd and his handlers-followers had unfurled the Quebec Liberation flag. It was to be his last smile of the night. He would waste none on the Sugar-man, who entered the ring to the shouts of the $20 patrons, sitting somewhere North of Moose Jaw in the upper reaches of the same Olympic Stadium where just four years before, Leonard had become the darling of the 1976 Olympics. Now, in his best laid-back manner, he bowed respectfully to all four corners—Nord, Est, Sud et Ouest—as the sounds of adulation fell like the cloudburst which had just drenched the 46,317 Fightophile fans who had turned out to see what was billed as the "Fight of the Decade," just six months into the decade. It was a build-up soon to be acquitted by the fight to follow.

But, if it did rain on the 46,000-plus, it was not to rain on Roberto Duran's parade as very shortly after the first bell it became evident he intended to dominate the action, and that Sugar Ray intended to allow him to do so.

The man who had subordinated so many other fighters to his own purposes rushed, bulled and grabbed inside, all the better to tie up the fast-moving Leonard and land his own body punches.

Before the fight, the fight mob had wondered about the selection of Carlos Padilla as the referee. His historic approach to a fight had been to break the two combatants whenever they got close enough to touch. Now, probably stemming from Ray Arcel's impassioned plea before the fight ("You're good . . . I only hope you let my boy fight his fight inside.") Padilla employed a "hands-off" policy, letting the bull bull and the matador get gored. It was Duran's kind of fight.

In the second, Duran bulled Leonard back to the ropes and landed one bonito right to Sugar's head. He then fell inside to follow up his advantage.

Round 3 looked much the same: Duran inside and Leonard landing underneath. But Duran was the aggressor at all times, aggressor being the operative word in the definition of "Macho."

By Round 4 Leonard, for the first time, held his distance and forced Duran back to the ropes. But the rest of the round—if not the rest of the fight—found Duran crowding in, following Arcel's directive "not to let Leonard do anything, to keep him up against the ropes." Dundee's advice to Leonard ("Slip in and out, in and out") went unheeded.

As the middle rounds progressed, both battlers went at it toe-to-toe. And even though this was Duran's type of fight, now Leonard was landing more often, and with more telling punches. The non-stop action—made even more non-stop by Padilla's refusal to break while there was anything resembling a loose hand showing—incited the fans to constant screaming, the Panamanian delegation shouting "Arriba, cholo" (or upstairs) and the Leonard followers shouting "Pour it on, Sugar."

Leonard was scoring, sometimes heavily underneath as he caught Duran charging in. Several times he landed his patented flurries and once even got away with an accentuated bolo. But it was Duran's aggressiveness that dictated—and, at times, even dominated—the fight, as he charged, pushed, punched and even butted Leonard in the ninth round.

Coming down the stretch, Leonard fetched many a good right solidly on Duran's "Macho"—and untrimmed—jaw. But all he got in return was a sneer from the Satanic-looking Panamanian, who then tore back into Leonard for more of the same. The pace and the noise continued unabated throughout the last two rounds, two rounds Duran conceded to Leonard, so sure was he now of his imminent victory.

When the final bell sounded, Leonard extended his hands in friendship. Duran, "Macho" to the end, did the only thing a Machoman could: he disdained them, walking past the man he hated with a passion that burned deep within him and throwing up his hands in exultation.

That exultation was premature, but correct. For when the decision was announced—148–147, 145–144 and 146–144, including 19 "draw" rounds amongst the three officials—Duran was the new "Champeon del Mundo" in as close and exciting a fight as boxing has ever seen.

Roberto Duran, as always unhumble in victory, said after the fight, "I proved myself the better fighter." His interpreter, Luis Enriques, boastfully added, "Duran over Leonard, (General Oma) Torrijos over (President) Carter and Panama over America."

And so, just as the Panama Canal passed to Panama in 1979, the welterweight title passed to Panama in 1980. Maybe that's what the two stars on the Panamanian flag truly symbolize: the blue for the waters of the Panama Canal and the red for the machismo of Duran.

For Leonard, there will be another day, another fight with Duran—Montreal Redux. And for that he'd better remember

Vince Lombardi's one underlying theory: "Winning isn't every-thing, it's the only thing."

Sugar Ray Leonard vs. Roberto Duran II
Superdome, New Orleans, Louisiana
November 25, 1980

It was as unbelievable as Santa Claus suffering vertigo, Cap-tain Kidd sea sickness, Mary having a little lamb. The "it" being Roberto Duran giving up, crying out "No más . . . no más."

The first time I saw machismo die a little came when, as a kid seated in the front row of the old Savoy Theatre in Washing-ton, D.C., I saw John Wayne kiss a girl instead of his horse. The second time came when Roberto Duran told the whole world to "kiss off" in the eighth round of his fight with Leonard.

Before that unmagic moment it was thought that there were but four immutable laws which governed the universe: That the earth goes around the sun; That lawyers always get paid first; That every action has an equal and opposite reaction; And that Roberto Duran would have to be carried out on his shield, blood streaming out of his ears, before he would ever quit. Now you can scratch one of the above.

It was an unthinkable act. As unthinkable as Ted Williams throwing away his bat with two strikes; as unthinkable as O. J. Simpson, unable to find a hole, suddenly stopping and falling down; as unthinkable as Secretariat or Alydar quitting at the top of the stretch.

Here he was, one moment the man who in another life would have notches in his gun rather than knockout victims on his record, the toughest hombre on the barrio block, boxing's noblest savage. And the next, a beaten man waving his hands in a cross between "Get lost" and "Something's wrong." But whose intentions were made perfectly clear by his repeated utterance of those deathless words "No más . . . No más," which translate, in any language, into "I give up!"

What had happened to turn the legendary "Manos de Piedra," the man without a heart and the sneering model of male machismo, into a quitter?

To understand the "why," first you must understand the "what." Boxing is a sport where everything comes in tidy little packages, is labeled and then put away. When something is divorced from reality, as the boxing fan perceives it, then it thwarts that desire to be pigeon-holed and filed away neatly. Boxing, more than any other sport—or human activity—puts full faith in its belief that the past is father of the present. However, in cases where there is no prologue, or it is illegitimate, with no history to rely on, then the moment is memorable, at best; controversial, at worst. Take the case of the Tunney–Dempsey celebrated "Long Count," or the Schmeling–Sharkey foul. Both were controversial because both pushed beyond expectable human experience and were inexplainable in any but new terms.

In a sport rife with memorable and controversial moments, few, in forthcoming years, will rival the moment when Roberto Duran called out "No más . . . No más," and held out his hands. There was no past experience for the boxing crowd to call on. And without that, they must resort to coming up with new answers to the perplexing question: "Why"—no matter how farfetched.

It soon became a field day for the so-called "experts." And the *Rashomon* theory put into practice—a reference to the classic 1950 Japanese movie in which four different people involved in a brutal rape and murder each give their own version of the crime. Each differing radically. So, too, did Roberto Duran's mysterious surrender become the subject of a long laundry list of theories. They, too, differ radically.

To many of the thousands of fans seated in the spacious Superdome—some, in the upper tiers, as far away as Hattisburg, Mississippi—and a large proportion of the millions watching on closed-circuit TV, the first thing which came to mind was the most popular three-letter word after "sex": the word "fix." But it was an unthinking, knee-jerk reaction, one neither thought out nor worthy of those who rendered it; a simplistic response to their hurt at not seeing their hero win or, more deeply, the cynicism that pervades today's society and thinks that all activities are pre-planned to take advantage of them.

However, while this writer will not deny that there have been such things as "fixes" in the history of the "Sweet Science," this was not one of them. For what purpose? Money couldn't have swayed Roberto Duran, inasmuch as he was set even before the first Leonard match. And, if, for argument's sake, "the fix" was in, how could one have been executed more clumsily or more inelegantly than merely waving one's gloves at 2:44 of the eighth round and crying out "No más . . . No más"? No, it wasn't a "fix." But boxing is a sport that suffers fools—and their reasoning—gladly.

Nor does the real answer to the question "Why" lie in the spoon-fed rationalizations that were handed out after the fight, all revolving around something called "stomach cramps." Hell, this was the same Duran who had fought the first Leonard fight with a bad liver and the flu. How could stomach cramps disable this man called "El Animal" by his followers? Especially when, supposedly rendered nolo contendre by those same cramps in the ring only an hour-and-half before, Duran hosted a big post-fight "Victory" party, eating and drinking like any other man who comports himself like Roberto Duran should—in an animalistic fashion. Most of the other theories are as airtight as domestic swiss cheese. Take, for instance, the supposed excuse that Duran had ballooned up before his rematch with Leonard and had to take off mucho weight in a short period of time. Granted that Duran had added more than thirty-three pounds living the easy life he had merited by winning the title in a hard-fought fight five months previous and had to find shortcuts to rid himself of all vestiges of easy living. Those searching for answers came up with several, all revolving around those supposed shortcuts to reducing his weight: Romantics cited "hard training," others "diuretics," and some even had the indelicacy to mention cocaine as an appetite suppressant. None of these explanations had ever been brought up before, although Duran had continually had to fight weight as well as opponents during much of his professional career. Why now? As a rationalization for the inexplicable behavior of Duran at 2:44 of the eighth round, that's why! But none bears up under the light of reflection; none qualify as answers for Duran's unfathomable act of quitting.

If these reasons don't wash, then the answer must be found elsewhere. For, as Agatha Christie's master sleuth Hercule Poirot was wont to say, "When a thing arranges itself so, one realizes that it must be so, (and) one only looks for reasons why it should not be so. If one does not find the reasons, why it should not be so, then one is strengthened in one's opinion."

Having looked at—and dismissed, for good reason—all other possible answers, one is left to look at the only place left: Roberto Duran's mind, one which apparently has more connecting locks than the Panama Canal.

All of which serves as a table-setting—albeit a long one—for the fight itself, billed as "Stone versus Sugar." It was the much-awaited rematch of the Montreal bout which already had been heralded as the twelfth greatest fight of all time in a recent poll.

Starting from the moment the bout was announced, Duran began to spew out his contempt for Leonard. "This time I will keel him," he was to say time and time again, attempting to belittle the man he had beaten in Montreal. And, to punctuate his remark as well as his dislike for the man he called "a clown," he would at times extend his middle finger in the half-peace sign. Other times, just to vary the act, his wife would extend the same pleasantries to Leonard's wife, Juanita. It was a family act with all the subtlety of a community bedpan.

Leonard, on the other hand, ignored his trainer—soon to become his ex-trainer—Dave Jacob's advice that such a rematch was "too soon" and that, instead of taking on Duran, he should take two warmup fights. Eschewing the warmup fights, and Jacobs as well, Leonard went into serious training to reverse the only defeat in his professional career—and recapture the crown he had come to look at as his own private property.

This time Leonard was determined, burning with the same intensity that had once burned deeply within the soul of Duran. He was also determined not to fight Duran's fight, not to let Duran dictate the pattern of the fight nor control the action as he had in Montreal. In short, Sugar Ray Leonard was prepared, which is more than Roberto Duran could say.

As the countdown continued and the crowds began to congregate in New Orleans—well-wishers and hangers-on alike, including some eighty-one Panamanians who followed Duran everywhere—something seemed to be amiss. The live promoters blamed it on everything from Thanksgiving to the football season. But a new element had been introduced to the equation: WBA champion Thomas Hearns. No longer could it be argued without fear of contradiction that the two best welterweights in the world were fighting in New Orleans the night of November 25th, 1980. However, at least one of the two best welterweights in the world showed up that night in the person of Sugar Ray Leonard. The other, Roberto Duran, looked like he was just playing through.

If there was one omen that was to foretell the outcome of the fight, it came at 9:01 CST, just before the fight actually started. For at that moment the Panamanian national anthem was rendered, sounding for all the world like the noise made by two gypsy wagons rolling over their own violins. It not only failed to stir the hearts of the twelve Panamanian hangers-on who had taken Duran's corner as a beachhead, but stimulated them to talk to each other and to anyone else they could find at ringside. That was followed by a boffo rendition of "America the Beautiful" by Sugar Ray's namesake, Ray Charles, which was to do for Sugar Ray what Kate Smith's "God Bless America" had done so many times before for the Philadelphia hockey Flyers. Round 1 to Leonard—and the fight hadn't even started.

Then came the opening bell. And Sugar Ray, wearing different colored trunks than he had sported in Montreal—black and yellow—soon began to show that he came equipped with other new trappings, including a new battle plan. This time, instead of leaving a wake-up call for Round 5, as he had in the first fight, he immediately moved out to the middle of the ring and landed the first punch, a left that caught Duran flush. After a brief moment when both tried out tentative left jabs, Duran put on one of his patented bull-rushes. But Leonard, instead of standing in harm's way, moved quickly backwards, out of reach.

It was like that for most of the first two rounds, Leonard moving out of the way and Duran barreling in. Occasionally Leonard would catch Duran to the midsection, coming under with uppercuts. But his battle plan seemed to be one of getting off first and his weaponry seemed to be a telling left jab, one that seldom missed. Duran would frequently respond by throwing his right—catching air most times and Leonard's left almost as often—and an occasional sneer.

As Round 3 began, Duran, who had missed more punches in the first two opuses than he had in his previous fifteen rounds against Leonard, became much more aggressive. He began mauling Sugar Ray into the ropes. But this time, instead of Leonard standing his ground, he either tied up Duran, caught him coming in or spun him off and moved out of danger. This time the pattern was different. And Duran's eyes began to tell more of the story than his fists as he stood in the middle of the ring, befuddled by the moth moving around the flame that burned within him, but never getting close enough to become scorched.

It was becoming woefully obvious to all but the most foolhearty Duran supporter that Leonard, who had gone to school for fifteen rounds in Montreal, was now putting in some postgraduate work—as well as some well-placed lefts. Instead of bullying Leonard to the ropes, Duran found himself shoved to the floor on one occasion, spun off on others and even suffering the ignominy of having his head pushed down, a la Ali with his opponents, on several more.

And then there was Leonard's movement of foot, something not seen since Fred last danced with Adele. By moving backwards and forwards, alternating direction and spinning Duran off continually—a strategy devised by trainer Angelo Dundee, who told Sugar Ray to "move 'em, spin 'em"—Leonard had Duran mesmerized. He followed Leonard's movements with his eyes, much like a beginning student would follow a foot outline at Arthur Murray's. And while he was watching, Duran was made to pay an entertainment tax, taking more than a few hard lefts to the nose for his efforts—or lack thereof. Between Rounds 5 and 6, Duran complained to his interpreter, Luis Enriquez, that something was wrong. Enriquez relayed the message to Duran's manager, Carlos Eleta, seated at ringside. But before Eleta's message, "Can he go on?" was relayed back, the bell had rung. Duran had a good round, negating most of the concern for his welfare.

Then came Round 7, one of the most memorable in the long history of boxing. It started out with Duran landing the first punch of the round for the first time in the fight. But that was to be the extent of his attack. For now Leonard, sensing that he "was in control" as he later was to say, began taunting Duran, first sticking out his chin and then his tongue. Duran looked at him with disbelieving eyes, unsure of how to handle this new threat. For the man who had been through 73 previous fights had met every threat head-on—punchers, runners, counterers, etc., but never taunters.

And, if that wasn't traumatic enough for Duran, he had yet to suffer one of boxing's most crushing and devastating psychological blows, a trick not dissimilar to a little kid's throwing one snowball in the air and catching the other kid looking at it with a second one, right in the puss. Leonard wound up with a mocking copy of Kid Gavilan's bolo punch. And while Duran stood transfixed, Leonard popped him a good one with his left. It was humiliating. It was worse. The man who had fought 441 previous rounds was made to look like a novice; like a fool. And many at ringside laughed. It was enough to make a grown man cry. Or quit.

That was the moment when a seed began to take root. And grow. And inspired Duran's act of submission sixteen seconds before the end of the eighth round.

For that was the moment Roberto Duran cried out, more in anguish and frustration than in resignation, "No más . . . No más." It was as if he had heard a mention of E.F. Hutton. Everything stopped. And with one contemptuous gesture, more of the "I'm-going-to-take-my-ball-and-go-home" variety than "I quit," he had, like the schoolyard bully who, when his prey ran, caught him, when he stood to fight, beat him, but when taunted, merely held up a middle finger and hollered, "So's your old man," or "Your mother wears tennis shoes." Only this time, the finger was encased in a glove.

It was a shame. A shame for Roberto Duran, whose seventy-three previous fights would be subjugated in memory to that one second when he cried out "No más . . . No más." A shame that a magnificent performance by Sugar Ray Leonard had to be tarnished and that his victory would be less than complete.

And it was a shame for the millions-upon-millions of people who idolized Roberto Duran, many of whom couldn't fill their bellies with food but had looked upon "Manos de Piedra" as someone who could fill their souls with hope, the hope of machismo. "No más."

But even though Roberto was to say "I fight no more" immediately after the fight, the realization and the magnitude of what he had done to his image and to boxing with that one gesture had not yet set in. It soon did. And rather than go home to Panama, where he had been a demi-god, he retreated instead to Miami, where he hid in seclusion for eight days.

There his conscience—as well as the advice of his manager, Carlos Eleta—began to play on him. He would come back, he announced, and as a form of penitence for his irrational act of telling everyone from Sugar Ray Leonard on down to "kiss off," he would donate his next purse to charity.

But if Roberto had told the world to "kiss off," the world was not quite ready to tell Roberto the same thing. And soon those who remembered Duran's daring exploits through seventy-three fights plus seven rounds began beseeching Roberto to come back, to wipe the only stain off his now somewhat tarnished escutcheon.

The president of Panama sent Duran a telegram which read, "You made Panama. You're our idol. Come home." Many others were to echo the words of El Presidente.

For Roberto Duran was a hero to millions, a living legend. And he had to come back one "más" time so that the permanent picture we keep of him in our mind's eye is not the shameful picture of a man who waved his glove desultorily in the direction of his soon-to-be conqueror, Sugar Ray Leonard—and by extension, in the direction of everyone who had ever lived vicariously through Duran's seething machismo—but of the warrior he once was. The warrior who once gave flight and fancy to man's machismo everywhere. The man Roberto Duran was in previous movies. For this he had to come back. To be Roberto Duran again.

Larry Holmes vs. Muhammad Ali
Caesars Palace, Las Vegas, Nevada
October 2, 1980

Sugar Ray Robinson sat paralyzed in his seat, tears welling up in his eyes. Scott LeDoux, head down, could only mumble, "I feel like they just shot my dog Spot." And thousands of others in the funereal surroundings of a parking lot outside Caesars Palace felt the same way. And worse. To them, it was as if both the Easter Bunny and Santa Claus had been destroyed. Muhammad Ali had lost.

In what was meant to be a religious revival for the Ali faithful, Muhammad Ali, who had already tied the *Guinness Book of Records'* mark for most miracles by a mortal—tying with Moses at two apiece—promised them yet another. And 24,790 made the pilgrimage to see the self-proclaimed "Greatest" do it again. But there was to be no "again." The clock had struck twelve. And Muhammad Ali, once the fastest afoot, the quickest of hands, had turned out to be a mere mortal. And an old, washed-up mortal at that.

His bag of tricks came up empty. The magic show was over. It was Carl Ballantine and Art Matrano "faking" it. He could no more come back than Houdini could come back from the dead after having told his followers he would.

Sure, he conned us. But, then again, when hasn't he? And it wasn't his fault. We wouldn't have been conned if we didn't want to believe. And we wanted to believe. Desperately. We were in on the "sting" because we were part of it. And we made Ali a 6½–5½ underdog at the end. It should have been Ali +28 points.

The fight? There was no fight. It was a futile left jab that never jabbed. A cocked right that never uncocked. A mysterious battle plan that never went into battle. And a legend that died.

For outside of the foreplay immediately prior to the fight— the only time he looked like the Ali of old—the Muhammad Ali who showed up for "The Last Hurrah" was merely the ghost of Ali past. A younger, tougher and better Larry Holmes "whupped" him in every which way, even charitably holding back several times or "accidentally" missing so that he wouldn't hurt the spectre that once was Ali standing directly in front of him.

Ali knew it was all over "after the first round." Some of the more faithful took additional time to come to the same conclusion; and even then, reluctantly. But it was painfully evident that "The man with the plan" had nothing. Larry Johnston, who had come all the way from Newark, New Jersey, left the arena after the second round. He couldn't stand it any more. "Ali put me through college," said Johnston, referring to the scores he had made betting Ali. "I grew up with him. I don't want to see him like this."

But see him they did. A pitiful hulk of a man who once was. By the end of the ninth round, when it was obvious he was defenseless, the referee, Richard Green, went over to his corner to inquire into his well-being. Ali and his manager, Herbert Muhammad, pleaded for just "one more round." And so, as the bell rang for Round 10, a bone-weary Ali came to the center of the ring, his eyes staring down in abject depression, his arms lowered to his side, his glories seemingly a thousand years past.

The tenth was no different than any of the previous rounds as Holmes drove him to the ropes, battered his already sore body, raked his puffed eyes and prolonged the misery by holding back right-hand shots to a by-now thoroughly unprotected midsection. The crowd was silent, as if at a wake, which is exactly what it was. Three more minutes of pure agony for Ali. And his faithful. Then the bell.

Green now hurried over to Ali's corner, concerned about the three-time champ's inability to defend himself. This time Angelo Dundee—the man who had pushed the-then Cassius Clay off his stool fourteen years before in the sixth round of his fight with Sonny Liston when Clay had wanted to quit with a "This is your night"—wig-wagged his hands. This was not his night. But, suddenly, Bundini Brown, refusing to believe that the party was over, pushed at Dundee. While the push was coming to shove, the third man in the corner, Pat Patterson, looked down at Herbert Muhammad for confirmation. Having seen enough, Herbert gave the time-honored signal for "cutting," which Patterson communicated to Dundee and Dundee to Green. Muhammad Ali looked up at Angelo and, through swollen lips, muttered "Thank you."

And so the man who had won fifty-six of his fifty-nine fights, had added the pelts of two seeming invincibles, Sonny Liston and George Foreman, to his belt and had given us many memories over the past two decades gave us one more: A defeated warrior sitting forlornly on his stool, going out with less a bang than a whimper. There would be no tintype in our mind's eye of his finish as there was of Joe Louis being knocked through the ropes by Rocky Marciano or of Jim Jeffries being beaten to his knees by Jack Johnson. Just a picture of another man grown old, a legend who had become mortal, sitting on his stool.

For Ali, unlike Louis and Jeffries, did not even try to return to his glorious days of yesteryear. That was the shame of it. His entire effort seemed to be concentrated on melting off some forty pounds-plus change from his Pillsbury Doughboy shape and showing us some of the same faces that had once captivated us coming from the face of a youth. Outside of those two efforts, Muhammad Ali was a mere mortal in the ring last October 2nd. And that was his biggest sin. The hopes and dreams of all our years were taken from us that night.

And Larry Holmes? What can be said of a man who was in what he himself called a "no-win" situation? He conducted himself—both as a man and as a boxer—as a champion. Holmes eschewed going to the body when going to the body might mean permanently hurting the man he, along with everyone else, idolized. He refused to degrade the man he had beaten afterwards, offering up an olive branch to "my brother, a great man." Larry Holmes was the only real winner on that October evening in a parking lot in Vegas. A man who invests boxing with a dignity it sometimes doesn't deserve, he deserves better than he has received.

This man can do it all. He now has eight straight knockouts in defense of his crown, tying Tommy Burns's all-time record. ("I'm gonna make Tommy Burns famous," he was to say before the bout.) He has done all that has been asked of him. And more. And he has done it better. It is his misfortune to come after the man who won the hearts of boxing fans everywhere.

Mike Tyson vs. Evander Holyfield
MGM Grand, Las Vegas, Nevada
June 28, 1997

> *The dog, to gain some private ends,*
> *Went mad, and bit the man . . .*
> *The man recovered of the bite*
> *The dog it was that died*
> AN ELEGY ON THE DEATH OF A MAD DOG
> —Oliver Goldsmith

Just when you thought you had seen everything—and I mean everything—in that Theatre of the Bizarre known as boxing, something happens that defies explanation. That "something" in this case was "The Bite Heard 'Round the World." Mike Tyson's inexplicable gnawing on Evander Holyfield's ears in their championship rematch last June 28.

Tyson had been underwhelming against Holyfield in November last year, his primary weapon of intimidation of no use against Holyfield, who gave much better than he got and took out Tyson with 273 or so lucky punches.

But the fight crowd, a crowd so cynical they could walk into a room of roses and look around for the corpse, thought Holyfield's one-sided ass-whuppin' was a "fluke," and when the rematch was announced, once again installed Tyson as a 7–2 favorite to reverse the drubbing he had received from Holyfield. To them, Evander Holyfield was anything but the "Real Deal." Tyson had merely underestimated him and since Holyfield had never put together two back-to-back great fights—or so the reasoning went—Tyson would assuredly recapture his pride and his title in the rematch.

The odds reflected an overblown assessment of Mike Tyson, who had lost the only two times he had ever been to the well—against Holyfield and Buster Douglas—and both times come back with an empty pail.

Moreover, his greatest win, the one which had earned him his reputation as an invincible warrior, a one-and-a-half minute dismantling of Michael Spinks, had been nine years before. Truth to tell, his prime was so far behind him, he couldn't find it in his rear-view mirror.

The other side of the coin was the underestimation of Holy-field, still disparaged as being a "blown-up cruiserweight." He seemed destined to be forever in Tyson's shadow, though his win in their first match had validated his credentials as the best heavyweight since Larry Holmes.

As the days dwindled down to a precious few before the scheduled May 3 fight, Tyson pulled out after suffering a cut eye in training and "The Sound and the Fury" was rescheduled for June 28 at the MGM Grand.

The extra time was supposed to give Tyson more time to train, to perfect the errors he made in the first fight—no combinations, no in-fighting, no jab, no defense, etc., etc., etc.—and to get acquainted with new trainer Richie Giachetti. It also gave him more time to mull over his devastating defeat at the hands of Holyfield and find excuses to explain it away.

Holyfield, on the other glove, just went about his business, training for the rematch, confident in his mind's-eye he could duplicate his victory and prove the first fight was, in his own words, "no fluke."

Two days before "The Sound and the Fury," the only sound and fury was that coming from Team Tyson, which objected to the selection of Mitch Halpern as the third man in the ring, as he had been in the first fight. What they should have done was object to Holyfield, not Halpern.

Team Tyson won their appeal when Halpern excused himself from the goings-on and the Nevada Athletic Commission filled his position with Mills Lane. It was to be a classic case of "Be careful, you might get what you wished for," as Mills would play a major role in the "Ear-Rie" events soon to take place.

The bell for Round 1 was barely audible through the din as Tyson came out of his corner tentatively, a departure from his usual freight-train-out-of-control running starts from his corner. After two minutes of clinching and wrestling mid-ring, Holyfield connected with a combination to the body and then with a left and a big right, hurting Tyson and driving him to the ropes. As the MGM Grand Garden crowd cheered for Holyfield, he continued his assault up to the bell. The first round was Holyfield's, the first time Tyson had ever lost a first round—in fact, twenty times he had never heard the bell ending the round, having ended his opponents' nights in that opening round.

The second round began as the first had, with Tyson coming out of his corner cautiously, almost too cautiously and throwing a wild, here-it-comes-ready-or-not left that missed badly. There is some blood over Mike's right eyelid which he continually wipes at, almost as if startled to find his own blood on him. Tyson looks at his corner, a little disconcertedly, then begins complaining to Mills Lane about what he perceives as a head butt. But Lane pays him no-never-mind. In a clinch, Tyson's head comes up as Evander's comes in, causing a collision and a deep gash in Tyson's eyelid. He again complains, but Lane tells him, it was "accidental." Holyfield begins shoving the smaller Tyson off in clinches and is warned by Lane as Tyson appears infuriated by Lane's refusal to intervene. End of round, another for Holyfield.

Now comes Round 3, one of the most infamous rounds in the long, infamous history of the sport of boxing. Tyson comes out of his corner without his mouthpiece, which Evander sees and signals both to Lane and to Tyson's corner, which corrects the omission. Tyson connects with a good overhand right and then, with more aggression than he's shown in the previous six minutes, connects with two right-hand leads. Holyfield begins to hold on, trying to blunt Tyson's attack. With a minute left, Tyson throws a good left and a strong left-right combination. Holyfield ducks under a Tyson hook and the two clinch.

What happens at this magic moment is open to debate. Not as to the actual happening, but as to the motivation. For as the two clinch, Tyson spits out his mouthpiece and gnaws at Evander's right ear, biting off a piece and spitting it out, onto judge Duane Ford's scorecard. Evander steps back and starts jumping up and down like Rumplestiltskin, as much in pain as in anger at Tyson's action. As he jumps away and turns his back, Tyson rushes him and pushes, not punches, him. Lane steps in between the two and tells Tyson, "That's one, another one and that's it," and takes two points away from Tyson—one for his biting and another for shoving.

After a four-minute hiatus, in which ringside doctor Flip Homansky comes into the ring to examine the damaged ear and determines it is cosmetically damaged, but that Holyfield can continue, Tyson continues to pace in his corner, much like a caged animal. Holyfield, standing in his corner, instructs trainer Don Turner, to "put my mouthpiece back in, I'm going to knock this guy out," and charges out of his corner. After two angry swings, the two again clinch, and Tyson again spits out his mouthpiece and this time bites Evander's left ear, evening up the score and the ears as well. After another few seconds, the round ends and Lane walks over to Tyson's corner and tells Tyson's corner he is "disqualifying" him—which Giachetti misinterprets, thinking Lane is stopping the fight because of Holyfield's inability to go on. At first Tyson screams, then rages out, in search of Holyfield, swinging at everything in his path, including two Las Vegas policemen who now have entered the ring to try to keep the peace.

Tyson is rabid, trying to get at everyone and anyone—especially Holyfield. But Holyfield and his entourage slip out of the ring. As a finally subdued Tyson is taken out of the ring, he jumps over seats trying to get at fans who are throwing things in his direction and taunting him, while the rest of the house stands in stunned disbelief.

Without pretending to be a psychiatrist without a license, Tyson's actions at making Evander "The Real Meal" can only be explained as his trying to get what he would later call "retribution" against Holyfield for his perceived head butting. And, having tried to invoke the help of Lane and finding he had no ally in the man his spokespeople had brought in to replace Halpern, decided to take things in his own hands. And teeth. Another explanation, put forward by Holyfield, was that Tyson, knowing he was losing both the fight and the battle of wills that went with it, had taken the easy way out. And still another had it that Tyson's bullying background and street style had him reverting to form.

Whatever, Tyson remained a man who had proven his bite was worse than his bark and will forever be known in boxing history not for his dominance of the division for almost a decade, but for having tried to make Holyfield into E-Van Gogh Holyfield.

Tyson, a man who has always been on the edge of falling into his own volcano, will forever be labeled. And although, in his dressing room, he continued to say, over and over again, "I'm through . . . I'm through . . . I'm through . . . ," he may not be through. Maybe Don King can get him a match with Hannibal Lecter.

Sugar Ray Leonard vs. Thomas Hearns
Caesars Palace, Las Vegas, Nevada
September 16, 1981

That blockbuster mentality that makes every fight sound like the Second Coming—and has given us enough "Fights of the Century" to take us through the era of Buck Rogers, 2400 A.D.—has now given us a lesser celestial happening called The Showdown. But a recent performance was lesser in name only; not in magnitude. No matter what they called the Leonard–Hearns to-do, it was one helluva fight staged in front of almost 24,000 recently-released mental patients who seemed collectively dedicated to the deafening of America. And, in the end, Sugar Ray Leonard acquitted the hype by soundly thrashing the supposedly invincible Thomas Hearns in a fight with more twists and turns than could be found in an early O. Henry potboiler. In so doing he laid claim to the undisputed welterweight championship of the world. As well as to a place among the all-time greats.

Leonard won more than just the fight. He won what Rodney Dangerfield, for lack of a more descriptive phrase, would call respect. Not only from his hard-hitting opponent but from hard-boiled sportswriters as well, many of whom had discounted Leonard's stock, belittling his accomplishments as part of a media buildup.

For ever since Leonard exploded on the media scene and on the national screen he has been regarded by many doubting Thomases, Jims, and Larrys as a media phenomenon. Maybe Howard Cosell, who had hitched his braggin' to a star, was the reason for the press downplaying Ray's abilities. But Howie knows a winner when he sees one, and Ray always had the makings of one. Nonetheless, "Forget it!" said the rest of the media, who continued to view Leonard merely as the greatest boxer ever to come out of Palmer Park, Maryland. Nothing more. It seemed that most of the boxing writers could never bring themselves to acknowledge that Leonard was as good as he was because that other, unspeakable medium, TV, found him first.

Or maybe it was the fact that Leonard was denied the ultimate satisfaction of destroying the man who had beaten him previously: Roberto Duran. Such triumphs, of course, had served as the anchor of so many other legends—Sugar Ray Robinson, who had turned the tables on Jake LaMotta, Randy Turpin, and Carmen Basilio; Muhammad Ali, who came back to "whup" Joe Frazier twice; Joe Louis, who destroyed Max Schmeling the second time around; Gene Tunney, who beat the only man who ever bettered him, Harry Greb; and Jack Dempsey, who almost came back to beat Tunney in the Battle of the Long Count. The centerpiece for each and every one of these ring worthies had been his comeback win over the man who had previously bedeviled him. All Leonard was remembered for was a desultory wave of a hand and the cry, "No más, no más." Of such things are legends unmade.

Moreover, according to many old-timers, for whom boxing goes in one era and out the other, there was only one "Sugar" and that accolade was reserved for one man and one man alone—Ray Robinson. (In fact, Robinson himself had tried to preserve that title of respect for himself in the face of other Sugars. One time, so the story goes, when Robinson faced another of the pretenders to the Sugar crown, George "Sugar" Costner, he reputedly told Costner during the prefight instructions, "Now I'll show you who's the real Sugar," and proceeded to prove his point by laying out Costner in one round. Afterward, Robinson chided the artificial Sugar with, "Now go out and earn yourself the name.")

But it was not only the press and the old-timers who denied Ray Leonard his rightful place. He was thrice denied, this time by the betting fans, who made Hearns a 6½–5 favorite.

And so it was that Leonard, seeking to rid himself of so many dybbuks, came to an inferno called a ring that hot airless night in Vegas wearing a robe emblazoned with the solitary word, Deliverance. It was an eloquent message that should have tipped off those who were supposedly "in the know" that Leonard was driven to exorcise the many demons that possessed him.

Yet the task facing Leonard was monumental. As was his opponent, the 6'-going-on-6'1½" Hearns, a legitimate welterweight with a heavyweight wingspan of seventy-eight inches—at least four inches longer than that of Leonard and longer still than many heavyweight champions. It was that reach, or so the reasoning went, that would allow Hearns to hold Leonard at bay, much as he had Pipino Cuevas, while setting up his lethal right hand. Hearns, however, was disabused of any such notions as Leonard slapped away his tentacle-like left time and again during the first two rounds. But while one of Hearns's favorite ploys was being negated by Leonard, Hearns was also defusing one of Leonard's, the tactic he had employed so successfully in the New Orleans fiasco—freaking out Duran with his mugging act.

For the first two rounds, the gladiators, who had apparently studied each other's playbooks, played with one another. Hearns, who chose to be introduced by the nickname the "Motor City Cobra," in preference to his more familiar moniker of "The Hit Man," acted more like a cobra than a hit man. Leonard's game plan was to circle the stationary cobra, first one way and then the other, in the manner of a mongoose, attempting to tire out the man who had gone more than four rounds only eight times in his entire career. And so it went, Leonard darting back and forth, his eyes transfixed in a fierce determination not to blink, almost as if held open by toothpicks, and Hearns resorting to long left jabs and an occasionally head-hunting right, most of which Ray avoided by pulling his head back Ali-style. The closest Hearns came to his tormentor was after the bell, when Leonard gave him a love-tap-cum-punch and Hearns clobbered him without turning the other cheek.

With Angelo Dundee's words, "Go out there and get him," ringing in his ears and a freshly-minted mouse beginning to erupt under his left eye, Leonard went out in the third to take the fight to Hearns. The first thing he took was a right to the jaw. And, surprise of surprises, he didn't even blink. Now he knew he could catch anything Hearns threw. The insight was heady as Leonard stood his ground and swapped shots with Hearns, who was fighting in one-punch combinations. For the first time, Leonard scored with his right and backed Hearns up; momentarily confused by Leonard's quick hand speed and agility, Hearns went on the retreat. At the bell, Leonard raised his hands in a victory salute. He now knew he would win, not merely that he could.

Rounds 4 and 5 mirrored the first two—sandwiched around Leonard's third—with Hearns pecking away at Leonard's angry-looking eye. But even in the face of Hearns's rapierlike left, Leonard was quietly moving inside with shots to the body. And, to the head, when he could reach the lanky WBA champion. Still, they were rounds for Hearns. Barely. But Round 6 was to change the complexion of the fight.

For the first time, Leonard, having taken control of the fight despite Hearns's elongated left, was now crowding Hearns. Moving inside. And, what's more, beating Hearns to the punch. More correctly stated, he was beating him to many punches. First it was Leonard's right over Hearns's low left; then it was a left over Hearns's equally low right. Suddenly, a wild left hook to the head caught Hearns's attention. And turned his head. As Ray's corner screamed, "Speed, Ray, speed," Ray obliged with a rat-a-tat-tat staccato. Suddenly the Hit Man was the Hittee Man, wobbling under a barrage of blows almost too numerous to count. But numbered among them was one punch in particular—a hard left hook to Hearns's unprotected rib cage—which caused the Cobra to grimace in pain. Its effects could not be appreciated then—it was one of a rapid-fire series of blows, as incapable of being severed from the rest as one pearl from a string—but one whose effects would be telling on Hearns. And, on the outcome of the fight.

Round 7 saw Leonard pick up right where he had left off, rattling more left hooks off Hearns's jaw than the Hit Man had experienced in his previous thirty-two fights. Over and over Leonard was to penetrate the would-be defenses of his spindly opponent, landing left hooks from in close as the crowd picked up the chant, "Leo-nard, Leo-nard. . . ." Hearns, unable to stave off the swarming Leonard and unable to tie him up inside, merely grappled to keep him away, pushing at his tormentor. And yet, as Hearns began to take on the appearance of a pinball, ricocheting from pillar to rope, he evinced that intangible known as courage, a rare commodity in any fighter and one that separates the greats from the near-greats. It worked to keep his unsteady pins under him.

At the end of the round Hearns staggered off in the vague direction of his corner, much the worse for wear. But Leonard also looked weary from his prolonged fungo practice, breathing heavily as he plopped on his stool. Later, Ray was to say, "I had him, but he didn't cooperate," which translated into, "I was arm-weary."

The eighth saw Leonard continue on the attack even as he wound down, with right leads and rights to the body in dutiful response to his corner's exhortations of "Body, Ray . . . Body, Ray . . ." Hearns, trying desperately to stem the seemingly inexorable tide that was all Leonard, attempted to catch Ray with a right. But, as the round came to a close with Leonard swarming in, he took off on his bicycle, throwing out his long left in a getaway manner. However, just as the fight had turned once, it was soon to turn again. Beginning with the bell for the ninth, Thomas Hearns reverted to the style that had seen him win 163 amateur fights, only eleven by knockout. Gone was the attempt to gain leverage by leaning in; gone was the low-held left and gone was the menacing Hit Man who instilled fear in the thirty-two opponents he had faced up to now. But gone, too, was the stationary target Ray had found so inviting. And, in its place, there suddenly appeared a masterful boxer, one who could finally take advantage of his seventy-eight-inch reach. It was the most startling role reversal since Edward G. Robinson played the leading man in *Woman in the Window*. The puncher had turned boxer and the boxer had turned puncher. And the puncher-boxer was clearly outpointing his supposedly faster opponent.

So it went through Rounds 9, 10, and 11, with enough rights thrown to count on your right thumb. Hearns was clearly dominating the action—what little there was of it as the high-rolling parishioners began clapping and whistling for more. But he was always just one punch away from "Queer Street," the street he had come down before, the pavement barely beneath his feet. But Hearns's befogged condition was not apparent. Not apparent to anyone, that is, except trainer-manager Emanuel Steward, who spent his time between rounds doing anything and everything he could to snap Tommy out of his severe case of mal-de-ring—up to, and including, shouting at his charge, "If you're not goin' to fight, damn it, I'm goin' to stop it!"

Somehow, Steward's shock treatment worked and Hearns came back. Strong. So, too, did his followers, and by Round 12 they had worked themselves up into a frenzy, with Hearns himself leading their vocal exhortations as their hopes took flight and form in roars of "Tommee, Tommee. . . ." No longer moving, Hearns came in on the one-eyed Cyclops who was stalking him, landing battering-ram lefts and rights to the body. It was Hearns's round. And his last hurrah, something even Hearns might have sensed had he been able to analyze his right-hand haymaker thrown at the half-blinded WBC champion, who somehow, someway, pulled his head back at the last instant.

Round 13, incredibly, saw still another turn in the tide of battle. Up off his stool came Ray, first pushing Hearns to the canvas as their legs entwined, then punishing Hearns with a right over a left and three left hooks to the head. Hearns tried mightily to hold Leonard off; unsure of how to clinch, he tried to throw a right. But Leonard beat Hearns to the punch, catching him and jarring him off balance. Another left by Ray, still another and a third, and suddenly Hearns was careening about the ring, his head rolling like a rag doll's, his motions uncoordinated. Leonard was atop Hearns as Hearns first leaned, then fell, into the ropes from a series of punches fired off too rapidly to count. Suffice it to say it was "Enough," as writer Vic Ziegel noted.

Finally, after a fusillade of rights the lanky Hearns, in his best imitation of an accordion, gently folded through the ropes. Referee Davey Pearl, who had ignored an obvious knockdown in the Larry Holmes–Earnie Shavers fight, deemed Hearns's exit from the ring more a fall than a knockdown—although they looked as if they were part of the same cause and effect—and told Hearns to "get up." As Hearns slowly reclaimed his feet and recollected his mind, trainer Angelo Dundee was up on the ring apron screaming, "Bullshit." Pearl motioned him down to his corner and looked back to find Leonard raking Hearns with another volley of punches, seemingly fired in a desire to prove something to somebody. This time he proved to Pearl that the Thomas Hearns leaning against the ropes on his haunches was knocked down by the collective force of his punches.

Pearl took up the count while Hearns tried to haul himself up to his six-foot, one-inch height, no easy chore and one which had the appearance of a balloon slowly inflating. Finally, Prometheus was unbound and Hearns was up, albeit unsteadily, as the count reached nine, just at the bell.

There seemed to be no doubt of the outcome now. At least not to 23,615 fans seated in the makeshift arena atop the tennis courts behind Caesars Palace. But the three judges, who undoubtedly had been watching tennis instead of boxing, still had Hearns ahead. Leonard was to make sure that there would be no disputed verdict. He wanted the welterweight title and went out to do it himself. He leaped off his stool at the bell for the fourteenth round—the longest Thomas Hearns had ever gone in a fight—and went right at Hearns, throwing rights and lefts as Hearns tried to avert them by twisting his body back and forth from a right-handed stance to southpaw and back again.

It was all to no avail as Leonard kept coming, throwing lefts to the body that made the exhausted Hearns wince and lefts to the head that made him blink. Finally Leonard landed his Mary Ann, a straight right to the chops, and threw up his hands in his traditional victory signal. But, miracle of miracles, Hearns wouldn't, or couldn't, fall and pitched backward into the ropes. Leonard wouldn't let him off the hook now and—between waving furiously to referee Pearl to stop the fight—raked Hearns with right uppercuts, left hooks, and hard rights. Still, Hearns wouldn't go down. But even if Hearns hadn't had enough, referee Pearl had. He pulled Leonard away as Hearns looked in his direction as if to quizzically ask, "Wha' happened?" and then reeled off in the direction of his corner, at 1:45 of the fourteenth round, the former WBA welterweight champion of the world.

At the press conference the next day, with both fighters sporting dark glasses and looking like Elwood and Jake Blues, Thomas Hearns was to show his respect for the "new champion, Sugar Ray Leonard. . . ." It was a long time acomin', but maybe, just maybe, Sugar Ray Leonard will get the respect he deserves. And, yes, Virginia—and Maryland, and all points north, west, and south—there is a new "Sugar Ray," on the boxing block.

THE CLASSIC FIGHTERS

SUGAR RAY ROBINSON

Any and all descriptions implying greatness can be applied to the man born Walker Smith in Detroit on May 3, 1921, but the one appellation that stuck was first uttered by writer Jack Case, who, witnessing for the first time a young lanky boxer fighting for the Salem Crescent Gym in New York, remarked to the manager of the team, George Gainford, "That's a sweet fighter you've got there." "Sweet as Sugar," replied Gainford for posterity. And so it was that "Sugar" Ray Robinson was born. Robinson came by the other part of his name honestly. Or somewhat honestly. For back in those days when the bootleg circuit-unlicensed fights held in small clubs held sway, the youngster originally went by his given name, Walker Smith—"Smitty" to his friends. One night "Smitty" borrowed the amateur card of a friend named Ray Robinson and became, from that night on, the man who would go on as Ray Robinson to become the greatest fighter, pound for pound, in the history of boxing.

No single label for Robinson is adequate. He was boxing's version of *Rashomon;* everyone saw something different. He could deliver a knockout blow going backward; he was seamless, with no fault lines; his left hand, held ever at the ready, was purity in motion; his footwork was superior to any that had been seen in boxing up to that time; his hand speed and leverage were unmatchable; on and on. There was an unaltered chemistry to Ray Robinson. He was magic; he was Hemingway's "Grace under pressure."

Robinson went unbeaten, untied, and unscored upon in his first forty fights, and it wasn't until his forty-first fight, against Jake LaMotta, that he was derailed, losing a ten-round decision. It was a decision he would reverse five times. Robinson went on to become welterweight champ, losing only to LaMotta in his first 132 fights, registering 84 knockouts.

HENRY ARMSTRONG

Henry Armstrong was a physical loan shark, a fighter who adopted General Clausewitz's theory that the winning general is the one who can impose his will upon the enemy. One hundred fifty-one times Armstrong imposed his will on his opponents, suffocating them in his swarming style, firing off his punches and then running over them, much like a runaway locomotive, with a ten-ton truck rumbling over their remains for good measure.

But the perpetual-motion machine might have been a mere footnote to boxing history had it not been for the fact that one of the members of his managerial brain trust was entertainer Al Jolson. And that Armstrong's greatest year, 1937, was also the year of Joe Louis. Until 1934, Henry Armstrong had been a struggling featherweight, fighting in and around Los Angeles with mixed results against opponents who remain almost as unknown as the soldier under the tombstone in Arlington. During one of the weekly Hollywood Legion fights, in front of a star-studded crowd, Armstrong distinguished himself, scoring a sensational knockout. Two of the stars, Ruby Keeler and Al Jolson, took a liking to the human hurricane and underwrote the purchase of his contract for their friend, Eddie Meade. All of a sudden his fortunes improved. And so did the caliber of his opponents.

WILLIE PEP

The man who scissored his given name of "Papaleo" into the palindromic "Pep" was boxing's version of the three-card monte player: Now you see him, now you don't. His movements, which took on the look of tap dancing with gloves on, left his opponents to speculate on their meaning and his fans to listen for accompanying music. Willie Pep fought as if he didn't like to get hit, having developed a great respect for his teeth at a very early age. He fought as a survivor, practicing a form of reverse polarity with the uncanny ability to anticipate an opponent's blows—and then parry them, pick them off, or just plain beat them with his own form of rat-a-tat punches. Throughout his long career, Pep substituted shiftiness and cunning for a lack of power, most of his knockouts coming not from a malicious blow but from his opponents falling to the ground in utter exhaustion, unable to keep up with the man labeled "Willie the Wisp"—soon to be contracted, like his own name, to "Will o' the Wisp."

Many of his opponents likened fighting the "Will o' the Wisp" to battling a man in the Hall of Mirrors, unable to cope with an opponent they couldn't find, let alone hit. Others compared the experience to catching moonbeams in a jar, or chasing a shadow. And yet another, Kid Campeche, said after a fight in which Pep had pitched a no-hitter, "Fighting Willie Pep is like trying to stamp out a grass fire."

Pep's greatest virtuoso performance came the night he gave the fans a run for their money, literally, winning a round without throwing a punch. His opponent on this occasion was Jackie Graves, a TNT-southpaw puncher with more than his share of knockouts. Pep had already tipped off a few friendly sportswriters that he would not throw a punch in anger during the third round. Despite their incredulity, they found that what happened was incredible. For Pep moved; Pep switched to southpaw, mimicking Graves; Pep danced; Pep weaved; Pep spun Graves around and around again; Pep gave head feints, shoulder feints, foot feints, and feint feints. But Pep never landed a punch. In the words of one sportswriter, Don Riley, "It was an amazing display of defensive boxing skill so adroit, so cunning, so subtle that the roaring crowd did not notice Pep's tactics were completely without offense. He made Jim Corbett's agility look like a broken-down locomotive. He made even Sugar Ray Robinson's fluidity look like cement hardening. Never has boxing seen such perfection!" Suffice it to say, all three judges gave Pep the round.

JOE LOUIS

Joe Louis's exploits are accorded no special place of prominence in The Ring Record Book. His 71 bouts are sandwiched between the records of James J. Braddock, whom he succeeded, and Ezzard Charles, the fighter he was succeeded by. Both Braddock and Charles had more professional engagements, as did Johnson, Dempsey, Tunney, Carnera, and Baer. And there have been men who had more KOs, Carnera and Charles; a higher percentage of knockouts in defense of their titles than Louis, Marciano, and Foreman; and more wins. But no heavyweight champion—and probably no sports figure—ever captured the imagination of the public, fan and non-fan alike, as the smooth, deadly puncher with the purposeful advance who, at his peak, represented the epitome of pugilistic efficiency. And no man was so admired and revered as this son of an Alabama sharecropper who carried his crown and himself with dignity, carrying the hopes of millions on his sturdy twin shoulders.

But the measure of the uncomplicated man they called "The Brown Bomber" cannot be found merely inside the ring. For, in a field devoted to fashioning halos, Joe Louis wore a special nimbus. And wore it with a special dignity.

Joe Louis used his words, as he did his punches, with a commendable economy of effort, saying a surprising number of things, and saying them in a way we all wish we had. There was his evaluation of his country's chances in the global confrontation with the Axis powers: "We'll win 'cause we're on God's side." Dignity. And there was his enunciation of his opponent's chances in the second Conn fight: "He can run, but he can't hide." Honesty.

MUHAMMAD ALI

Part showman, part promoter, and all champion, Muhammad Ali was boxing's version of the Pied Piper, always heading up his own parade with a band of admirers in his wake as he rolled through the sixties and the seventies. Coming on the scene when the heavyweight championship—if not all of boxing—was just a rumor, this man-boy who answered to the name of Cassius Marcellus Clay for the first part of his life proved that charm travels as far as talent as he became the most celebrated and flamboyant figure in the world of sports in merely three years. Clay-Ali strutted with the air of a carnival midway performer and considered fame his due—so much so that he took a sword and dubbed his own shoulders "The Greatest," a title many of his followers were willing to concede to him after he twice destroyed a supposedly invincible Sonny Liston. Adding verbal footwork to his amazing agility in the ring, Ali brought a touch of the theatrical to boxing, his doggerel making his opponents' heads spin as much as his fast hands.

Everything had a name or a meaning: His opponents were called "The Bear," "The Mummy," "The Washerwoman," and "The Rabbit"; his moves were "The Ali Shuffle," "The Rope-a-Dope," and "The Anchor Punch." And all became part of the language of fistiana. He even took to predicting the rounds when his opponents "must fall," and he rarely welshed, delivering the results almost as reliably as the newspaper.

Ali made great copy with his wonderfully engaging remarks, calling Leon Spinks, "So ugly that when a tear runs down his face, it only gets halfway down and then runs back . . ." Or, in answer to whether he was scared of Sonny Liston, "Listen, black guys scare white guys a lot more than black guys scare black guys." But it was one of these off-the-cuff remarks that came back to haunt him and short-changed "The Greatest" of almost three years of his career when he was still at the peak of his talents.

ROBERTO DURAN

Just as at one time the universal way for a woman to proclaim ownership over a man was for her to pluck some invisible thread from her man's lapel, Roberto Duran also had a way of proclaiming ownership over his opponent: storming straight into the chest of his opponent and leaving a devastating punch to the liver as his calling card. Roberto Duran was the quintessential warrior, a predatory fighter who epitomized the Spanish word meaning "courage and aggressiveness": machismo. Fighting with a conscious will to destroy, this street kid from the ugly barrios of Panama City fought every fight with the remembered resentment of his childhood—his cruel eyes burning brightly with contempt for anyone crossing his path; his teeth biting into his mouthpiece in a half-sneer, half-smile; his burning desire to own his opponent, body and soul. He had the look of an assassin and the assassin's conscious will to destroy.

The one-time shoeshine boy fought the first 24 fights of his career in the steamy, hot flyblown cauldrons that passed for fight clubs in his native Panama, rendering 21 of his 24 opponents into instant walking obituary columns. Some were also-rans who also ran, others up-and-coming fighters who gave flight until no longer possible and then were destroyed by the man who was then becoming known as Manos de Piedra, or "Fists of Stone." But Duran viewed them only as stepping-stones to the top, his sadistic street upbringing permitting him no remorse. Time and again his prefight oration would consist of "I will show him, I will keel him." (Later, after he had won the lightweight championship, he would glance at the mortal remains of a former challenger named Ray Lampkin being carted off to a hospital on a stretcher and announce on television in a deadly derringer tone, "The next time I send him to the morgue.")

JACK DEMPSEY

William Harrison "Jack" Dempsey was, purely and simply, the greatest fistic box-office attraction of all time. And, not incidentally, one helluva fighter to boot. If Dempsey's opponent could walk away after a fight, it was considered a success. So great was his punch that some 60 of them, including those he met in exhibitions, never walked away after the first round.

Dempsey was the perfect picture of the ring warrior. Approaching his opponent with his teeth bared in a mirthless grin, bobbing and weaving to make his swarthy head with the perpetual five-o'clock shadow harder to hit, his black eyes flashing and his blue-black hair flying, Dempsey took on the look of an avenging angel of death.

His amazing hand speed and lethal left hook, combined with an anything-goes mentality bred of necessity in the mining camps of his youth, made every bout a war with no survivors. He used every possible means at his disposal to win, his definition of survival less a breaking of the rules than a testing of their elasticity—hitting low, after the bell, behind the head, while a man was on the way down, and even while he was on the way up. "Hell," he said, "it's a case of protecting yourself at all times."

But Dempsey never had to, his opponents did. After having spent several years outboxing the local sheriffs, Dempsey came out of the West with a fearful record, a nickname, "The Manassa Mauler," and a manager named Doc Kearns, who was to play spear-carrier to Dempsey's greatness. With an animal instinct, an inner fury, and a lust for battle never before seen, Dempsey blazed a searing path through the heavyweight division. After dispatching contender Fred Fulton in just 18 seconds in July of 1918, Dempsey proved he was no one-fight phenomenon as he followed that up with a 14-second knockout of former "White Hope" claimant, Carl Morris. Now all that stood between "The Manassa Mauler" and the heavyweight crown was a small mountain of a man by the name of Jess Willard. But after one puerile left jab, Dempsey whipped over his meal ticket, his left hook, and left a dazed Jess Willard on the floor, his jaw shattered in seven places, his dreams of retaining his title just as shattered.

JACK JOHNSON

Nobody knew just how good Jack Johnson really was, including Jack Johnson himself. Never bothering to combine delusions of grandeur with delusions of honesty, Johnson lived as he fought, unpredictably. A clever, scientific boxer the size of all Galveston, Johnson could move around the ring as gracefully as a cat, catching punches with his elbows, his hands, and the upper portions of his arms—in the words of Damon Runyon, "No greater defensive fighter than Jack Johnson ever lived." Or time his blocks and parries to set up his opponent for alternate right or left thrusts to the head, all done with the ease and speed of a featherweight. Like a bullet, each one of his gloves had someone's name written on it. Unfortunately he would rarely pull the trigger, fighting each fight as if he were merely cruising on his batteries, using little or no energy, all the while smiling his sweet smile of inscrutability. To assess Jack Johnson's place in boxing history is as difficult as attempting to categorize Shakespeare's Othello merely as a Moor. And as misleading. The rise and fall of Jack Johnson was shaped as much by his being black as by America's reaction to it. And in many ways his was as much a preordained tragedy as that of Othello.

Denied his chance to find his roots in big-time boxing, Johnson blossomed in bootleg fights, called "Battle Royals"— a barbaric pastime in which between six and eight fighters, all blindfolded and all black, would fight until the last man left standing was adjudged the winner—and on the Chitlin' Circuit against other blacks. Isolated in their own fistic world, some black heavyweights gained a measure of celebrity: Sam Langford, Sam McVey, Denver Ed Martin, and Joe Jeannette, to name but a few. But few got further than that. Jack Johnson was to defy one of boxing's ineluctable verities: that no black man could ever become the heavyweight champion of the world.

Johnson menaced the heavyweight division like Tamerlane the Tartar and his yellow hordes had menaced the populace in the fourteenth century, beating the likes of Bob Fitzsimmons, Bill Lang, and Jim Flynn and other white heavies. Finally, the man the papers called "the Playful Ethiopian" tracked the titleholder, Tommy Burns, down to Australia, and there, more by dint of pleading and wheeling and dealing than by shrewd negotiations, Johnson got his long-awaited opportunity.

MICKEY WALKER

"Mickey Walker will best be remembered as the middleweight who had the best left hook and the biggest thirst in the business." So spoke Jim Murray, one of sports' most puckish writers. "If it hadn't been for the one, the thirst, the other, the hook, might have made him the only 155-pound heavyweight champ in modern history," Murray opined. Correctly. In that Era of Wonderful Nonsense, when the all-enveloping hand of Prohibition was on the land, somehow Mickey Walker slipped through its fingers. Together with his manager, the fun-seeking Doc Kearns—who, at the suggestion of Damon Runyon took over the managerial reins of Walker after his first manager-mentor, Jack Bulger, died, thereby becoming, as one writer noted with tongue in cheek, "Damon to Walker's Runyon"—the Magnificent Mick made a little cause for celebration go a long way. And in doing so made a small fortune out of a somewhat more substantial one.

Between drinking enough to keep twenty speakeasies busy and training for fights by getting the proverbial "shave and a haircut," Walker covered more fistic ground than any man in modern boxing history. His fistic ambitions knowing no weight bounds, he alternately fought elephantine opponents and defended his two titles in his spare time. "Sober or stiff, I belted the guts out of the best of them," Walker boasted.

And he did, too, as he came barreling into an opponent, squinting through arms crossed in front of his face and ceaselessly hammering enough bruising, bonecrushing left hooks to the body to set their ribs afire. Called the "Toy Bulldog" by Francis Albertanti because of his ferocity and tenacity—and "A Miniature Jack Dempsey" and "A Larger Edition of Terry McGovern" by those with an eye for fistic comparisons—the incomparable Walker looked the part, his puggish nose and accumulating scar tissue over his eyes giving him the droopy-eyed look of a bulldog. But, truth to tell, Walker fought more like a bull terrier than a bulldog. It was almost as if his between-round exhortation from Kearns had been "Sic 'em" as he attached himself to his opponent and never let go, worrying his opponent as a terrier would a bone.

GENE TUNNEY

It has been said that great fighters are born, not made. But you can't prove that by Gene Tunney. Nor his success. Gene Tunney was clearly an artist with predecessors—other fighters whose styles and genres he appropriated and adopted. Coming to the sport without the basic physical equipment of the greats before him, Tunney became a one-man laboratory for the analysis of strengths and weaknesses of fighters, his own and his opponents. He drew on the style of that prince of the middleweight division, Mike Gibbons; sparred for a moving picture short with the master boxer of all time, James J. Corbett; and listened to Benny Leonard's advice on how to beat Harry Greb. He then mixed and braided their input into an independent and eclectic talent that made him a winner, one who got there through sheer willpower.

Gene Tunney's claim to greatness lay not in his two fights with Jack Dempsey, but instead, in his five fights with Harry Greb, "The Human Windmill."

Having returned from the Great War with the A. E. F. light heavyweight championship pinned to his Marine Corps khakis, Tunney depended on the ring for his livelihood, making himself available to any promoter worthy of his salt who would ballyhoo him as "The Fighting Marine" and wrap him in the red-white-and-blue to artistically cover up his lack of a record. For the better part of a year Tunney kept himself in a state of perpetual preparedness, campaigning against never-wases, has-beens, and fighters who weren't even household names in their own households.

After a cameo appearance on the undercard at the Dempsey–Carpentier fight, Tunney got his first big chance—challenging the swashbuckling Battling Levinsky for the American light heavyweight championship. Tunney won, going away, literally, in 12 rounds. His first defense, some four months later, came against the aforementioned Mr. Greb and was hardly family viewing. Greb destroyed Tunney in a bout that Grantland Rice said looked like "a butcher hammering a Swiss steak." The fight, a classic in How to Foul, commenced with Greb rushing Tunney and butting him squarely in the face, fracturing Tunney's nose. While Tunney tried to stem the flow of blood down his face, Greb held Tunney's head with one hand and with the other used Tunney's unguarded face as a punching bag. By the end of the third, Tunney was literally wading in his own blood. And by the end of the fight, he looked like a second-place finisher in an abattoir. His body sore, his face a mess, Tunney was convinced that if Greb couldn't finish him off, he was a better man than Greb. And set out to prove it.

Nine months later Tunney went back in against Greb to win back his title and avenge the one stain on his all-winning escutcheon. The nine months proved to be a proper gestation period for Tunney as he gave birth to a plan of attack, aided and abetted by the greatest ring scientist of all time, Benny Leonard, who taught Tunney how to come in under Greb's overextended elbows with body punches under the heart, all the better to take the steam out of Greb. The lesson took, and Tunney gained his revenge—and his championship. But Tunney was possessed of an obsession, Jack Dempsey, and he made the man-tiger, then the heavyweight champion of the world, his own personal Everest.

ROCKY MARCIANO

Noah Webster defines the word determination as "a strong resolve; the quality of being resolute or firm in purpose." But then again, Mr. Webster never saw Rocky Marciano fight. It would have lent an entirely new dimension to the word. Christened Rocco Francis Marchegiano, the man known as "The Rock" hardly had an auspicious ring beginning, fighting, and knocking out, one Lee Epperson in three rounds in March, 1947. Little could anyone then appreciate that Epperson would be the beginning of one of the most memorable streaks in the annals of sports, the first of 49 straight victims Rocky Marciano would notch on his belt before he hung up his gloves. But before Marciano would face his second opponent, some 16 months later, he would take his somewhat more than limited skills to New York to sculpt them into those of a fighter.

He was fortunate to find Charlie Goldman, a miracle worker who performed the alchemy of turning the piece of rock into Rocky Marciano. As Goldman told it, "Marciano was so awkward we just stood there and laughed. He didn't stand right, he didn't throw a punch right. He didn't do anything right."

But under Goldman's competent eye, and with his own sense of destiny, Marciano dedicated himself to becoming a fighter. And more, a champion. Fed a steady diet of stiffs, he stepped over their prone bodies on his way up the boxing ladder of success, continually honing his half-polished skills.

Determined now to become "Great," with a cap "G," Marciano worked diligently with Goldman on the bare-bones rudiments of jabbing, hooking, basic footwork, and other such basic boxing mechanics, spending untold hours in isolation. But one thing Goldman wouldn't touch was Marciano's power punch, his right hand, called the "Suzi-Q." It was one of the most devastating weapons ever brought into a ring and Goldman wanted to preserve it in all its unadulterated purity and power.

The combined work of boxing's version of Pygmalion and Galatea wrought one of the most brilliant success stories in fistic history. Once nothing more than a semblance of a fighter, by the sheer force of his will and the skills of his trainer Marciano now stood astride the heavyweight division, ready to battle for the championship.

As indestructible as any fighter in history, Marciano walked into, and through, thousands of hard, clean, jolting shots in the manner of a human steamroller, wrecking his opponents with baseball-bat swings to the arms, the midsection, the head, and just about anything else within reach. Always ready to take two or three punches to land one, the determined Marciano melted down the guards of his opponents, and with the shortest arms of any champion in the history of the heavyweight division, hewed them down to size.

JULIO CESAR CHAVEZ

To understand boxing one must first understand its roots. From its very beginnings, the sport has resonated with ethnicity. First it was the Sons of Erin, then the Sons of Mendoza and the Sons of

Italy who fought their way up the fistic ladder to gain a foothold into society. Next came black fighters who had fought in fistic obscurity, their fight for recognition thwarted by racial prejudice. And finally, it became the turn of the Latino fighter, especially those Sons of Montezuma from Mexico, who took their place in boxing's center ring.

At first the number of Mexican fighters, like Bert Colma and Baby Arizmendi, was but a trickle, the list of others who followed their lead in the first five decades of the twentieth century so few their names could be written on a postcard with a description of the picture on the other side of their Mexican hometown and more than enough room left over for an over-sized postage stamp and their return address.

By the late '60s, fighters with mellifluous-sounding Latino names like Romeo Anaya, Ricardo Arrendondo, Miguel Canto, Chucho Castillo, Rafael Herrera, Ruben Olivares, and Clemente Sanchez had entered the ranks of boxing and attained stardom, followed by Pipino Cuevas, Carlos Palomino, Lupe Pintor, Salvador Sanchez, Alfonso Zamora, and Carlos Zarate in the '70s. The trickle became a Niagara in the decade of the '80s, so many that the bookkeeper's mind rattled at the sheer number of Mexican greats. But in any itemized inventory, only one name begins and ends all such lists for Mexican boxing fans: the name of Julio Cesar Chavez.

Chavez was such a deity in his native Mexico that his very nickname, "J.C.," as in Julio Cesar, might give you a small hint of his revered status. Described as a "legend" and a "superstar," two words so rarely used to describe fighters you have to look them up to make sure of their spelling, he was nothing less than a national monument, his entry into the ring greeted with all the shuffles and ruffles of a patriotic event—complete with flags, buntings, banners, and the expectations of his countrymen.

The legend of Julio Cesar Chavez started on the night of February 5, 1980, when, his face still a stranger to the razor, the 17-year-old Chavez knocked out someone or other named Andres Felix in six. However, the legend was almost over before it began, Chavez recalling, "I felt I did not want to fight again . . . I left the ring that night thinking that it was for the last time. For one thing, I didn't get paid."

But within the month the young Chavez was back in the ring and fighting in and around his hometown of Culiacán, with an occasional side trip to Tijuana. Facing an assorted group of nonesuches, most looking like they had just emptied out the mission house, he ran up an unblemished record of 43 wins, 36 of those by knockout.

BARNEY ROSS

Ring historians can trace the lowest point in boxing's fortunes back to the year 1933. Attendance and gate receipts had hit an all-time low, and the heavyweight champion was Primo Carnera, at best a joke. Nat Fleischer, venerable publisher of *The Ring,* was moved to write, "I dare venture that 1933 is the worst on record." If boxing had been a wake, it would have been an insult to the deceased. It had nowhere to go but up, and that "up" would be in divisions other than the heavyweight division which had quickly become the sandbox of boxing. There were "To Let" signs in five of the other seven traditional boxing classes as well. If there was to be a revival it would have to be sparked by the only two divisions that had sustained interest in their continuity and their championships, the welterweight and lightweight divisions. And led by the one man who had, by now, given life to both: Barney Ross.

A great fighter is always before his time. Or after it. Barney Ross was his time. For not only was this graduate of the Chicago Golden Gloves and Maxwell Street ghetto the vehicle used by Mike Jacobs to start his 20th Century Sporting Club—initiated informally with the annual Milk Fund fight in 1934, an over-the-weight match between Ross, then the lightweight champion, and the Fargo Express, Billy Petrolle—but in the thirties, when men fed their bellies with hope rather than food, he served his supporters a healthy portion of ethnic pride.

In the era when descendants of Daniel Mendoza so dominated the sport—with four champions at the beginning of the thirties and identification with the Sons of David so prevalent that Max Baer took to wearing the Star of David on this trunks, even though he wasn't of the faith (trainer Ray Arcel putting the lie to whether Baer was Jewish said, "No he wasn't, I saw him in the shower.")—spokesman Joe Humphreys was to write, "The United States today is the greatest fistic nation in the world and a close examination of its four thousand or more fighters of note shows that the cream of the talent is Jewish." But if they dominated the sport, one man dominated their talent, decimating half the Jewish pugilistic population. That one man was Jimmy McLarnin, a heavy-handed battler who, not incidentally, added insult to injuries by being Irish.

ARCHIE MOORE

Archie Moore is proof positive that boxing builds character as well as characters. At an age when most men are already planning what to do with their Social Security checks, Archie Moore finally got what had been a long time in coming: the light heavyweight championship. But the road to that championship had been paved with detours and plenty of hard knocks. Born in either Collinsville, Illinois, or Benoit, Mississippi, on either December 13, 1913, or December 13, 1916—depending on who was keeping score, Moore or his mother—Moore was either 36 or 39 when he won the light heavyweight crown. Asked about the discrepancy in his birth date, the quick-witted champion sidestepped and countered, "I have given this a lot of thought and have decided that I must have been three when I was born." Moore's first bout came in 1935 against the picturesque-sounding Piano Mover Jones. His pay for the night was the small coins collected in a hat that was circulated amongst his fellow CCC camp members. The result was a knockout, the first of more than any boxer in history would record.

For the next 17 years, with time out for a severed tendon in his wrist, acute appendicitis here, a perforated ulcer or an organic heart disorder there, Moore treaded the highways and byways of America in search of recognition and an elusive title shot—boxing's version of the bridesmaid, always lining up first to be second. Just another of the many talented "colored" fighters trying to break into the big time, Archie had to go through a lot of back doors so that the black fighters of today could go through front doors, fighting in bootleg battles, tanktowns, and small clubs on the Chitlin' Circuit. Hardly one to suffer in silence, he responded to his second-class treatment with the only means available to him: his fists. And with hopes blowing on those fists to keep them warm, he scored knockout after knockout.

Moore survived where few others could have, and 17 years and 110 knockouts after Piano Mover Jones, he stood on the threshold of his greatest dream: the light heavyweight championship of the world. On December 17, 1953, he finally achieved that dream, decisively beating Joey Maxim for the title. But even then Moore got the fuzzy end of the lollipop, earning only $800 for climbing into the ring and to the pinnacle of his profession as well. However, in the strange and wondrous way of boxing, Moore got something more than merely the championship belt and $800; he also got Maxim's manager, wily old Doc Kearns, the man who had guided Maxim—and before him, Jack Dempsey and Mickey Walker—to the title.

SUGAR RAY LEONARD

Many old-timers, for whom boxing goes in one era and out the other, believe that there was only one "Sugar" and that the accolade was reserved for one man and one man alone: Sugar Ray Robinson. In fact, Robinson had tried to preserve his title in the face of a fistic avalanche of "Sugars." One time, so the story goes, when Robinson faced another of the so-called pretenders to the Sugar crown, George Costner, he reputedly told Costner before the fight, "Now I'll show you who's the real 'Sugar,'" and proceeded to prove his point by laying out Costner endwise in one round. Afterward, Robinson chided the artificial Sugar with, "Now go out and earn yourself the name!" But another "Sugar," Ray Charles Leonard, was to earn himself the name. And with it a place in history.

Starting back with the 1920 Summer Games in Antwerp, when Frankie Genaro traded in his Olympic gold medal for the championship gold of professional boxing, the Olympics have been a shortcut to fistic gold and glory. Throughout the intervening years several gold medalists have translated their Olympic victories into successful professional careers and even championships, including the likes of: Fidel LaBarba, Jackie Fields, Otto von Porat, Pascual Pérez, Floyd Patterson, Pete Rademacher, Nino Benvenuti, Cassius Clay, Joe Frazier, Chris Finnegan, and George Foreman, to name but a few. But no one Summer Olympics gave us more champions who turned in their amateur trinkets for professional treasures than the 1976 Games in Montreal. And no one fighter ever capitalized on his Olympic gold more than the darling of the 1976 Olympics: Sugar Ray Leonard.

In a day and age when the new buzzword among Madison Avenue executives was "charisma," Sugar Ray Leonard, with his infectious boy-next-door personality, was someone who possessed what Clara Bow had a half-century before, that indefinable trait called "It," for lack of a better word. Highly marketable and properly packaged, Leonard became a commercial property before he ever stepped into a professional ring.

But Sugar Ray Leonard was to acquit the buildup and raise it some. For when he came upon the scene, the welterweight division, if not all of boxing, was merely a rumor, its ranks depleted in a sort of boxing's version of Gresham's Law, with bad fighters forcing out good ones.

JAKE LAMOTTA

Jake LaMotta. His very name evokes memories of a fighter who had no passing familiarity with the canvas; "The Bronx Bull," who brought the strategy of "playing possum" to life, charading as a beaten fighter one second and then, the trap sprung, coming back to life to catch a surprised opponent with a devastating fusillade the next; the only fighter to beat Sugar Ray Robinson in the Sugarman's first 132 fights; and the man who incensed some of the more sensitive boxing fans by admitting to a Senate subcommittee that he had thrown a fight to Billy Fox. Jake LaMotta was all these things—and more. He was a throwback to the old barge fighter, one for whom every fight was a war with no survivors taken; a rough-and-tumble fighter who gave every fan his money's worth; and a fighter whose name was never taken in vain when words "art" or "science" were employed. He was, indeed, "The Raging Bull," and that was the basis of his fame.

But LaMotta was a curious piece of goods as well. His fists—messengers of some outlaw corner of his psyche—were as delicate as those of a concert pianist, forcing him to eschew the head and direct his attack almost exclusively to the body. His heart was that of a Thoroughbred trapped inside the body of a mule. His body was that of a short, squat fireplug, physically full enough to qualify as a light heavyweight or heavyweight— both of which he had been in his earlier amateur life—and yet housing a full-fledged middleweight. And his style was that of a street kid, no subtlety, no finesse, just straightforward, unabashed balls-out slugging.

To LaMotta, fighting was a personal statement. He fought with an anger that seemed as if it would spring forth from the top of his head like a volcanic eruption. And yet it was just this crowd-pleasing, bull-like style that made Jake LaMotta a negotiable commodity. And made LaMotta popular. Together with Jake's "knock-the-stick-off-my-shoulder" approach to boxing was his style—or lack thereof. In a fighter a stance is as expressive as a punch. With his legs fully planted—as if they were glued to the floor—and spread like the Colossus of Rhodes to support his massive frame, LaMotta challenged anyone to knock him off his pins. Even in the face of Sugar Ray Robinson's onslaught in their sixth fight, famously known as "The St. Valentine's Day Massacre," there was no unconditional surrender by LaMotta to undeniable facts. He withstood the assault and stood upright on legs that were strangers to him, absorbing Robinson's barrage like a sponge. One could almost hear the sound of metal fatigue as the ironman sagged and crumbled but never fell.

EMILE GRIFFITH

Madison Square Garden is at once a building and a symbol. But it was not always thus. Originally a New York, New Haven & Hartford Railroad freight yard and depot, the structure had been converted in 1874 by none other than P. T. Barnum into a magnificent hall called the Great Roman Hippodrome. That first night the 15,000 curiosity seekers who crammed into the Hippodrome were treated to a veritable Circus Maximus: Arabian horses, waltzing elephants, cowboys and Indians, tattoo'd men, chariots driven by women, fire-eaters, and just about everything else imaginable—and some things not. Three incarnations and 94 years later, the fourth Madison Square Garden opened its doors to the public for the first time with a boxing double feature: Joe Frazier–Buster Mathis and Emile Griffith defending his world middleweight crown against Nino Benvenuti in front of some 20,000-plus fans. This was only fitting, Emile Griffith having fought more main events in the Garden—Gardens III and IV— than any other headliner in history.

But to call Emile Griffith merely a "house" fighter is to do an injustice to one of the foremost scrappers of all time. For not only had Griffith settled permanently into boxing's mecca, but he had also settled into the hearts of its fans as well.

In his prime he was a "Y"-shaped youngster with a pinched waist and shoulders big enough to support water buckets, with a sparkling style of fighting to match the sparkle that danced and played in his dark eyes. Moving around the ring with all the grace of a ballet dancer, he would employ his formidable right and snaky left, which snapped out like a towel popping—pop! pop!—to maneuver his opponent into a position where he could corner him.

One horrible night he maneuvered his opponent, Benny "Kid" Paret, into a corner and, unhinged by "mean sayings by Paret," avenged an unendurable insult with a homicidal assault. Afterward the normally happy-go-lucky Griffith, still smoldering like a volcano at Paret's slings and slurs, could only say, "A man who wants to fight for the title must gamble." Paret did, and lost, both his title and his life in a miscalculated gamble that cost him everything.

GEORGE FOREMAN

In any listing of great comebacks, the finger of history lingers longer over the name of George Foreman than any figure in boxing—nay, all of sports. For this fugitive from the law of averages made dust out of conventional wisdom by coming back after a ten-year layoff to win the heavyweight championship 21 years after winning it the first time. And, in a turnaround worthy of a Harvard B-School thesis on how to change your image, reinvented the George Wheel by transforming his image from that of the winner of the Sonny Liston scowl-alike contest to that of a cuddly teddy bear.

Like Gaul, Foreman's career could be neatly divided into three parts. The first began in 1968 when the former dead-end kid from Houston's Fifth Ward's mean streets and recent entrant into federal Job Corps program used his crude strength to overwhelm Soviet finalist Jonas Cepulis in two rounds to win the Super Heavyweight gold medal at the Mexico City Olympics and then paraded around the ring holding a tiny American flag in celebration. Turning pro the next year, Foreman ran off a string of 37 consecutive victories over some of the heavyweight division's most well-unknown names, dissembling 34 of them into smaller, neater pieces with his ponderous punches, delivered in the manner of a man hewing down trees. All of which earned him a shot at the reigning world champion, Joe Frazier.

Preparing for his fight with Frazier, Foreman watched films of the champ and soon discovered that "he only knows one way to fight . . . he comes at you straight ahead and wide open." And so it was that the first time Frazier rushed in, Foreman hit him with a thunderous left which sounded like that of an explosion felling six or seven bystanders. And Frazier as well. That was the first sound heard. The second was ringside commentator Howard Cosell's by-now famous call, "Down goes Frazier . . . Down goes Frazier." It was to be the first of six times Cosell would utter that phrase as Frazier took on the look of a bouncing ball, once even lifted up in the air like a tree trunk being pulled from its moorings. Finally, after the sixth knockdown, Foreman called to Frazier's corner, imploring them to "Stop it . . . I don't want to kill him." But even if Frazier's corner hadn't had enough, referee Arthur Mercante had, and stopped the one-sided ass-whuppin' at 1:35 of the second round.

George Foreman had won the heavyweight title. But he had won more, also being crowned with the title of "Invincible," a title he added oak-leaf clusters to with two quick knockouts of challengers King Roman and Ken Norton in defense of his title.

But even though Foreman was now viewed as the equal of the man Jack had met at the top of the beanstalk, having taken out his last eight opponents in two rounds or less, one man, trainer Angelo Dundee, insisted, "My guy will stick him, hit him with straight shots and pick him to pieces." That "guy," of course, being Muhammad Ali.

BILLY CONN

Whenever shall we see the likes of a Billy Conn again? A feisty, brash little leprechaun who fought every fight with all the bravado of somebody going down aboard an ocean liner, humming "Nearer My God to Thee . . ." Billy Conn was the prototypical Irish sprite, a charmingly raffish character with an elfin grin and a puckish stance; so elfin, in fact, that if ever a fighter could tug at a forelock with his gloves on, Conn would have been the one to do so. Bringing to the ring all the blarney and headstrong qualities of the "auld sod," this more spectacular version of Tommy Loughran was able to weave castles in the air with his fists and leave trails of gold with his fistic triumphs, spun over the greats and near-greats of the late thirties with his skills as a clever fighter. What very few remember about this little kid with the honest hustle, who started as a skinny, elbowy welterweight and worked his way to the cusp of the heavyweight championship, is that along the way he worked his way through the boxing alphabet, taking the measure of no less than ten men who held titles at one time or another—from A to Z: Fred Apostoli, Melio Bettina, Young Corbett III, Vince Dundee, Solly Kreiger, Gus Lesnevich, Babe Risko, Teddy Yarosz, Tony Zale, and Fritzie Zivic.

Never fed a schedule of stiffs, Conn took them all on, beating them with his speed afoot, his agility of hand, and the balls of a cat burglar. In one fight, local Pittsburgh rival Oscar Rankins floored Conn early in the fight with a straight right. Conn arose and, through the fogbanks of memory, proceeded to bang out a ten-round decision. Afterward he apologized to his manager Johnny Ray for "getting knocked out," still not knowing he had won. That was Billy Conn, an artistic practitioner who always got the job done.

JOE FRAZIER

The roots of Joe Frazier, like those of almost every other successful boxer, were literally planted in economic deprivation. Born in a one-room shack on a small farm, Joe grew up in dirt-poor poverty, picking radishes for 15 cents a crate to help his father, who had lost his left arm in an automobile accident. "I was his left hand," Joe said. "If he had the hammer, I held the nail." And for the majority of his adult life, Joe Frazier would use that same left hand to hammer his way to fistic greatness. But if chance hadn't twice lit up like a small electric lightbulb in a small room the size of the farmer's shack of his youth, it is doubtful if Joe Frazier ever would have risen to the heights of greatness he achieved.

His first big chance came when Buster Mathis, the only man ever to beat Joe as an amateur, hurt his hand before the 1964

Olympics, and Frazier, an alternate, stepped in to represent the United States, doing Uncle Sam proud by bringing home a gold medal from Tokyo. Returning to his adopted city of Philadelphia a hero, Frazier repaired home to nurse a broken thumb and a bruised bank account. Once again, on the borderline of poverty, he took a job in a slaughterhouse waiting for the chance to turn pro and for his thumb to heal. Finally a group of Philadelphia businessmen put together an athletic corporation called "Cloverlay" to underwrite Frazier's career and in August of 1965 he turned pro with a one-round knockout over Woody Gross.

Frazier won his next 14 fights as well, his straightforward, all-businesslike style—punctuated by his deadly left hand—taking out 13 of his opponents within the allotted number of rounds. And then chance again lit up, this time in the form of Muhammad Ali, who refused to step forward for induction on April 18, 1967. Within scant hours, boxing's pooh-bahs and political chest-thumpers had defrocked Ali, taking away his title, scattering the heavyweight title like crumbs to the wind. Almost immediately every Tom, Dick, and WBA rushed in to fill the vacuum in an "Ali, Ali, All in Free" fashion, advertising for anyone and everyone to campaign for the right to ascend to Ali's throne as heavyweight champion. Joe Frazier was one of those who threw his left into the ring.

EVANDER HOLYFIELD

The story of Evander Holyfield is an updated version of The Little Engine that Could—the story of a man who could no more be discouraged than ice welded nor steel melted. Exuding those essential oils of dedication and determination, he constituted a majority of one who thought that whatever he undertook could be done, and that was all it took. It was almost as if you could hear him saying, "I think I can . . . I think I can . . ." with every challenge faced and every punch landed.

Evander always believed he could, no matter the number of denials or rebuffs. Taken by his mother to the Atlanta Boys Club at the age of eight, the 65-pound youngster became fascinated by the speed bag but was told by the boxing coach, Carter Morgan, that he couldn't hit the bag unless he joined the team. And so it was that denied his request he joined the team where he would soon become known as "One-Punch" Holyfield, because, as he would recall, "I stopped guys with one shot—Boom . . . But then you didn't knock them out. You'd hit them hard enough for them to cry and the referee'd end the fight."

But one punch wasn't enough when, at the age of 11, he lost to the first white opponent he ever faced, one Cecil Collin, and went home to tell his mother he no longer liked boxing and wanted to quit. But his mother, the source of his spiritual guidance, told him she had "not raised a quitter," and that he could quit only after he had beaten Collin. The scene would be repeated again; again he would lose to Collin and again he would go home and tell his mother he no longer wanted to box, and again she would explain that quitting in defeat was not acceptable and sent him back to the club yet again. And when circumstances had so arranged themselves that he would face Collin a third time he not only won the fight but also gained a belief in himself that he could do anything he set out to do.

LARRY HOLMES

It was almost as if the biography of Larry Holmes began with Chapter Two. For here was a 28-year-old boxer laboring in the virtual anonymity of boxing's vineyards and backyards, undefeated, untied, and unwanted, when chance—in the form of the WBC and Don King—singled him out to fight for the so-called heavyweight championship. And therein lies a tale with all the elements of intrigue found in a best-selling novel. The two alphabet-soup organizations known as the WBA and the WBC had parasitically attached themselves to the underside of boxing in the early sixties. By 1978, they had begun to suffocate boxing with their favoritism of promoters, countries, and matchmakers, taking money under the table, around the table, over the table itself and, in some cases, even taking the table for rating fighters and dispensing championships in the same cavalier manner a party girl hands out her phone number to everyone with the right connections. One of those with the right connections to the WBC was promoter Don King.

What King had was an option on a Muhammad Ali–Ken Norton rematch. What he didn't have was a contract for the upcoming Leon Spinks–Ali rematch, Spinks having beaten the memory of Ali in February of '78.

Undoubtedly, there are a few traditionalists remaining who are committed to the romantic and honorable notion that championships are won and lost in the ring. However, WBC president Jose Sulaiman was not amongst their number. In Star Chamber proceedings held in a smoke-filled room Sulaiman defrocked Spinks of his hard-won mantle and conferred it on Ken Norton—only because Warren Harding was unavailable— coronating him the WBC heavyweight champion without a title fight. Promoter King, still in possession of an option on

"Champion" Norton's services, with the blessings of the WBC, set up a "title" defense for Norton against Larry Holmes, a loyal member of King's court.

Larry Holmes was boxing's version of the "Forgotten Man." Even with 26 straight wins and 19 KOs, the only way he could have gained recognition would have been if he had walked into a masquerade party backwards wearing his birthday suit posing as a burnt Parker House roll. His only TV exposure had been an eight-round decision win over Tom Prater as part of Don King's ill-fated U.S. Boxing Tournament. In the shower of heavyweight gold all around him, Holmes had nothing to hold but a pitchfork. And his connection with Don King.

MIKE TYSON

To perplexing questions like "Why does Hawaii have interstate highways?" and "Why did kamikaze pilots wear helmets?" can be added another: What the hell happened to boxing's kamikaze pilot, Mike Tyson? Before Fate let Tyson close enough to touch the hem of her skirt, he was, as he described himself, "a poor black heading in a direction . . . I don't know where," earning his stripes in advanced thuggery on the mean streets of New York's Brownsville section. That "where" soon became, courtesy of the State of New York, the penal institute for incorrigibles in upstate Johnstown. It was there that an instructor, with the eye of a recruiting sergeant, picked the young tough out of the herd and recommended him to the attention of veteran manager Cus D'Amato, who had guided Floyd Patterson and José Torres to world titles many years earlier. D'Amato took the youngster under his crusty wing, filling the empty 5-foot-10-inch, 200-pound vessel with his unique philosophies and values in an attempt to sculpt him, a la Henry Higgins, into his next great boxer.

The alchemy began to pay dividends, although not immediately, as the young Tyson, enchained in his own insecurities, could not translate D'Amato's teachings into practice. Teddy Atlas, then working as Tyson's trainer, remembered the night in Scranton when Tyson, fighting the local favorite, floored his opponent twice in the first round only to see his fallen opponent get back up. Coming back to his corner after the first round Tyson tried to beg off, complaining, "I'm tired." Atlas pooh-poohed his charge's whine and sent him out for the second, a round in which Tyson inflicted more of the same on his outclassed opponent. Again, at the end of the second Tyson returned with an excuse. "Think my hand's broken," said the disheartened Tyson. Atlas, trying to dole out crumbs of comfort, told Tyson he was winning even if he hadn't put his opponent away, and sent him back out for the third and final round with a "Get out there . . ." verbal shove. After one more round of serving up the same punishment, Tyson was awarded the decision and thanked D'Amato and Atlas for getting him through a moment that could have short-circuited his career.

JOHN L. SULLIVAN

John Lawrence Sullivan. The very name brings back memories to that rapidly dwindling number of fight fans whose fathers saw this bull-like man club opponents into the earth with an awesome right and told them about his exploits. To the average adult, he is a storied figure in boxing history who gave color to his age, somewhat in the fashion Babe Ruth and P. T. Barnum gave color to theirs. To the younger generation, he is merely a name, spoken in reverential terms by elders and used as a benchmark for modern boxers like Joe Louis and Muhammad Ali.

THOMAS HEARNS

Their names are as indelibly etched on boxing's landscape as the faces on Mt. Rushmore. They are the eleven men who have accomplished boxing's version of the "hat trick"; those who have writ large their names as masters of all they surveyed in three different weight classes. Those triple champions, in order of their winning their third title, were: Bob Fitzsimmons, Tony Canzoneri, Barney Ross, Henry Armstrong, Emile Griffith, Wilfred Benitez, Alexis Arguello, Roberto Duran, Wilfredo Gomez, Thomas Hearns, and Sugar Ray Leonard.

Now one of those eleven, Thomas Hearns, has scaled his own personal Everest, a hill from which he can look down on the other ten three-time winners as the only man ever to win world titles in four different weight classes.

For those who may have taken up residency alongside Rip Van Winkle and do not recognize the greatness that is Thomas Hearns, let us backtrack for a second and give you a quick thumbnail of the man they call "The Hit Man." Thomas Hearns looks like a fighter built by committee. From the wrists to the shoulders, the committee has dictated he be heavily muscled, possessing the physical build of a wide receiver, complete with shoulder pads, and, with a seventy-eight-inch wingspan, the look of a basketball center. They gave him huge hamhock hands, all the better to make his opponent one with the resin. But this quasi-heavyweight upper body sits atop a slender thirty-inch waist poised on spindly, praying mantis-like legs, giving him the appearance of someone who works in an olive factory dragging the pimentos through. But to his opponents, this six-foot-one-inch string bean—his shadow further lengthened by his achievements—looks just like the man met at the top of the beanstalk. And just about as dangerous.

OSCAR DE LA HOYA

Ask any boxing fan the definition of the word "welterweight" and they'll stare at you with the eyes of a meditative fish. Even that most punctilious of wordsmiths, Noah Webster, drawing on his fine command of the English language, comes up empty, explaining it in his tome as deriving "prob. fr. 'welt': to thrash, beat."

But if the definition of the term "welterweight" is lost to etymologists, so too are the many who have toiled in the 147-pound vineyard, their efforts hidden under the twin bushel baskets of the heavyweight and middleweight divisions and commanding less attention than the international trade balance.

While many of the greats and near-greats in the welterweight catalogue of constituents have begotten no more than a small lake of print around an islet of illustration, several have been able to step forward, center stage, and stir the boxing fan. And the press.

Usually those rare moments when the welterweight division becomes the center of the boxing world's attention come when the heavyweight division is on the cusp of being called off on account of lack of interest, the fans turning their attention elsewhere while waiting for action, any action, to erupt amongst the heavies—a theory no doubt related to some hypothesis about the watched pot.

Jump-skip, dear reader, to the early '80s when, again, the heavyweight division had become about as exciting as the sight of paint drying and fans looked elsewhere to feed their boxing fix. They found it in the welterweight division, its ranks filled to overflowing with the likes of Sugar Ray Leonard, Thomas Hearns, Wilfred Benitez and Roberto Duran. Once again the division came front and center, pulling boxing out of its doldrums.

And now, today, as the heavyweight division grinds down to a bore-snore, its so-called headliners either too old in the tooth, too pacifistic or not even household names in their own households, it is the welterweights who again breathe life back into the old sport—giving it so much that its very breath could becloud a mirror.

This time around, it is its two superstars—not only of the welterweight division, but of all of boxing—Oscar De La Hoya and Felix Trinidad, who have made the welterweight souffle rise yet another time. Together these two warriors give one of boxing's most overlooked divisions the recognition it so richly deserves. And so rarely receives.

THE HISTORY OF BOXING: THE WAY OUT

I

To understand boxing one must understand its roots. From its beginnings, the sport has resonated with urban ethnicity, drawing its recruits from the tenements, the ghettos, the projects, the barrios, the "nabes," places that offered little presence and even less of a future. Many a troubled and troublesome youngster has embraced "The Sweet Science" as a way out, a social staircase out of the mean streets that formed his limited world, fighting his way, bloody hand–over–bloody hand, up the ladder of acceptance the only way he knows: with his fists.

It has always been thus. The trail began in the back streets of London slums and led to the teeming tenements of a young America where a new species of ruffian was first admitted to full fellowship in street battles and then turned its hands to boxing.

Ring archaeologists trace America's boxing roots back to the late 1840s when American politics and pugilism formed an unholy alliance of skull breaking and skullduggery. By the end of the decade, millions of Irish immigrants had fled their native land in the wake of the Great Potato Famine and arrived in America carrying only a valise of hope. That hope was soon thwarted in a world run by the hated White Protestant Establishment. Everywhere they encountered signs reading "NINA," meaning

"No Irish Need Apply." They turned to the only world left open to them, the world of politics. The result was the most powerful and corrupt political machine ever known: New York's Tammany Hall. Tammany—which had built its political structure on the dual cornerstones of bullying and bribery—took to hiring thugs, all handy with their dukes, as "immigrant runners," so-called "gentlemen" who welcomed newcomers right off the boat and guided them to secluded spots where they would either be swindled or induced to vote the straight Tammany ticket. In the opposite corner, so to speak, were the "toughs" employed by the Native American Party, equally adept at using their fists. Dubbed the "Know Nothings" because of their practice of answering any and all questions with "I know nothing," this anti-Catholic party was formed to counter what they viewed as alarming waves of immigrants flocking into America, particularly from Ireland. Dedicated to keeping the despised "Harps" "in their place," the Know Nothings frequently resorted to force.

It was inevitable that there would be wars between the camps. Not so inevitably—and yet natural still—the antagonists would become America's first pugilists. Among those with Tammany stripes were such thugs-cum-fighters as John Morrissey, Lew Baker, James Turner, and "Yankee" Sullivan, while the Know Nothings could call on the likes of Tom Hyer and Bill Poole. Prizefighting was then regarded as nothing more than an unlawful activity engaged in by outcasts, a furtive trade carried out in secluded spots, often taking place in the back rooms of saloons or on river barges or in rings pitched in the pine, usually one step ahead of the local constabulary.

Challenges and fists began to fly in equal proportions as Tammany and Know Nothing toughs faced off in continual brawls. When the dust had cleared, one man, John Morrissey, stood as the best of the motley lot. After meeting every assault hurled in his direction, Morrissey retired from combat and, slipping white gloves over his grotesquely misshapen fists, turned to the world of politics, becoming a prominent figure in Tammany and twice winning a seat in Congress. He became a very wealthy man, establishing lucrative gambling houses in New York City and at Saratoga Springs where he built the famous racetrack that still stands, monuments to his successful escape from his ignoble roots.

In the two decades after Morrissey retired, other Irish fighters—many, like Morrissey, from the Auld Sod—began to fight their way up the fistic ladder. It would remain for one fighter, however, to embody the Irish spirit and their battle to kick over the traces of their second-class status: John Lawrence Sullivan.

By the 1880s, cocksure and confident of its future, America was casting about in search of national heroes to tie its patriotic kite tail to. In those politically incorrect days when men were men and women were damned glad of it, the man most men wanted to be was this swaggering, boastful bully boy called everything from "The Boston Strongboy" to "His Fistic Highness" to "The Prizefighting Caesar" to "The Great John L." to just plain ol' "Sully."

This American tintype was tailor-made for the lusty era in which he fought. Meeting President Grover Cleveland, Sullivan challenged established protocol by extending his burly paw in the direction of the president and booming, "How are ya, Boss? Sure glad to shake your hand." Cleveland loved it. So too did Sullivan's legion of fans, many of whom made shaking the hand of John L. the highlight of their lives. Untold thousands extended theirs proudly to others proclaiming the catchphrase of the era: "Shake the hand that shook the hand of the Great John L."

In a day when the world got all its news via two channels, the while-you-get-your-hair-cut weeklies and word of mouth,

John L.'s exploits monopolized both, his legend continually increasing in range and breadth with every telling and retelling. And the stories, all propped up with reverential anecdotes—his "I-can-beat-any-sonuvabitch-in-the-house" chest-thumping challenge to one and all, his week-long benders, his romances with the Bloomer Girl of the Month, and, of course, his many triumphs in the ring—didn't end at the twelve-mile limit. His supporters, many of whom were Irish and for whom he had become the symbol of their own struggle, swept blarney off its feet.

Sullivan continued to write legend with his fists, devouring opponents as easily as he did food and drink. One opponent remembered nothing of his battle with John L. other than that Sullivan's awesome right "felt like a telephone pole shoved against me endways." Another said, "It felt like the kick of a mule." Wins over Paddy Ryan and Jake Kilrain—in the last championship bareknuckle fight in boxing history—earned him the title "Heavyweight Champion of the World" in the eyes of the boxing community and "The Strongest Man in the World" in the minds of his fans. But John L. turned his back on the ring and his attention to the stage, choosing instead to tour the country in a vehicle tailor-made for his own meager talents entitled *Honest Hearts and Willing Hands*.

Catcalls rained from the balcony while calls for Sullivan's return to the ring poured in from everywhere else. In indignation, Sullivan took pen in hand to issue a written proclamation. It read, in part: "I hereby challenge any and all bluffers to fight me for a purse of $25,000 and a bet of $10,000. The winner of the fight to take the entire purse. First come, first served." Ignoring the black man Peter Jackson, perhaps the one most deserving of a shot at the title, he invoked his own version of a "Color Line," listing three potential challengers whom he labeled "bluffers." The third of these was James J. Corbett, who had, Sully proclaimed, "uttered his share of bombast." He added that "the Marquis of Queensberry must govern this contest, as I want fighting, not footracing." He signed the letter, "Yours truly, John L. Sullivan, CHAMPION OF THE WORLD," in capital letters, befitting its author.

The first to come forward and post good-faith money was the third of the aforementioned "bluffers," James J. Corbett, practitioner of something he called "Scientific Boxing." Despite Sullivan's prolonged layoff and bloated condition—John L. had not fought in thirty-three months and weighed some thirty-five pounds above his normal fighting weight—he was still installed as a 4–1 favorite by the "sports" to beat his challenger.

The fight was held on September 7, 1892 at the Olympic Club in New Orleans. It was really no fight at all. For twenty rounds Corbett gave an exhibition of his "Scientific Boxing." Moving briskly but never urgently, Corbett would give the champion a come-hither look, but never be at home when Sullivan came calling, remaining safely out of range of Sullivan's wild right-hand swings, leaving the champion growling and thrashing about the ring like a wounded bear. Finally, in the twenty-first, by now as weak as day-old ginger ale and winded by his vain pursuit, Sullivan stopped stock still in the middle of the ring and demanded that his opponent come and fight. Corbett obliged him, answering the taunt with his own right hand, driving Sullivan to the canvas face first. As he lay there being counted out, his fans in the gallery quickly began to rid themselves of their Sullivan colors, throwing down their green banners upon the stricken gladiator until they covered the ex-champ like a shroud.

When he finally groped his way out from under his colors, Sullivan turned to his second, lightweight champ Jack McAuliffe, and asked, "What happened?" With tears in his eyes, McAuliffe told Sully the awful truth: he had been knocked out. Grasping the significance of having fought into the Indian Summer of his career, the unsteady Sullivan, helped to the ropes, firmly grasped the top rope and spoke to the assemblage: "The old man went up against it just once too often. He was beaten . . . but by an American." And then he ended with his usual flourish, "Yours truly, John L. Sullivan."

The torch had passed, not only to an American, as Sullivan had proclaimed, but to an Irish-American. And yet Sullivan's legion of fans was not about to pass on their adulation to the man who had humiliated their hero. In a case of illogical free association that could only be explained by Professor Rorschach toppling over his inkwell, Sullivan's Irish-American fans scorned their hero's conqueror, calling him derisively, "Pompadour Jim," and "Gentleman Jim," in obvious reference to his effete and foppish style of dress. In several cities, gangs of Irish toughs took out their frustration by waylaying anyone rash enough to admit they had bet on or even rooted for Corbett, Irish-American or no.

To them, and to Irish-Americans everywhere, John L. Sullivan was the holder of the original copyright as the first great Irish-American hero. No imitators need apply, thank you. Just as he had battled his way up the ladder of success, his non-boxing brethren were battling their own way up. In the process they would become policemen, politicians, and part of the middle class. In a real sense, they were fulfilling their hero's legacy by exiting their enforced positions as second-class citizens in a society that promised that all men were equal.

More Irish-American fighters would follow Sullivan's lead, with Irish-Americans enthusiastically embracing them. One old story, told by cauliflower tongues of the time, tells of the fight between Peter Maher and Tom Sharkey at the Lenox Club in New York back in 1897. It seems that feelings were running high between the rival camps backing the combatants. One old fellow, a townsman of Maher back in Galway, sat in the balcony over-looking the ring waving an Irish flag and proclaiming to everyone within earshot what his boy would do to Sharkey, offering to bet all kinds of money that Maher would "knock Sharkey kicking" with a single punch. When the men had taken their places in the ring, Charley Harvey, the announcer, advanced to the center of the ring and began the usual prefight ritual: "In this corner," he roared, without benefit of megaphone, "we have Peter Maher of Galway, Ireland!!!" At that the old Irishman began cheering wildly, waving the banner bearing the proud harp of his homeland and slapping everyone in the vicinity on any part of the anatomy available to him. "And," continued Harvey, "in that corner is Tom Sharkey of Dundalk, Ireland." The old Irishman now sat quietly in his seat. After a few seconds, he turned to his neighbor and said, "So Sharkey comes from Ireland, too, does he? Sure 'n I thought he came from Australia. . . . Well, if that's the case, I don't give a damn who wins!"

Much as the old Irishman was confused by the entry of a new "player," so, too, were thousands of other Irish fans who cheered for their "own." Or fighters they thought were their own. So powerful was the Irish hold on boxing that it now became fashionable for fighters to adopt Irish names in the belief that it was the only way to make their "name" in the sport, even if it wasn't their own name. And so it was that boxers whose surnames were Piaga, Goldberg, Carrora, Anchowitz, and Giordano hid behind names like Young Kid McCoy, Kid McGowan, Johnny Dundee, Charlie White, and Young Corbett III, and on and on. It began to look like, as the old Irish saying made popular by Rudyard Kipling put it, "The colonel's lady and Judy O'Grady [were] sisters under the skin."

Until this time, the Irish had had an all-but-exclusive hold on boxing. Now others began to make inroads. They came from the same background as their predecessors, the ripe fruit of tenement-house growth, particularly those warrens on the Lower East Side of New York where, according to journalist and social reformer Jacob Riis, "12,220 of the 32,390 buildings classified as tenements" could be found. And most of those battling their way out of the tenements were Jewish, sons of the second great wave of immigrants.

The first great fighter to come out of the Lower East Side was Leach Cross who was, in reality, a dentist whose given name was Louis Wallach. Like so many others of the time, he adopted a nom de guerre, and an Irish-sounding one at that. Wallach-Cross was a lightweight who began fighting in 1906 and was soon taking on the cream of his division: Jem Driscoll, Packey McFarland, Tommy Murphy, and Dick Hyland among others. Leach Cross was something else as well: the first real Jewish sports hero, important enough to be the first athlete ever to appear on the "front page" of *The Jewish Forward*. (As sportswriter Barney Nagler once pointed out, the *Forward* was the only paper you read backward; reporters would run in with late-breaking news hollering, "Hold the back page.")

In becoming the first real Jewish sports hero at the end of the first decade of the twentieth century, Cross supplanted another "Jewish" hero, baseball pitcher Christy Mathewson. Although non-Hebraic, Mathewson inspired thousands of Jewish mothers, unable to keep their first-generation American sons from playing America's Pastime, to hold him up as a beau idol. They were hoping against hope that their sons would at least pattern themselves after the great New York Giant superstar who, not incidentally, had gone to college and played chess.

"Leachie," as his fanatic followers called him, popularized boxing among the many Jewish fans who would never have followed the sport were it not for him. And his success not only blazed a trail for other ghetto gladiators, but gained respectability for the Jewish community, much as the Whitechapel district of London had been the beneficiary of the ring success of the great eighteenth-century bareknuckle champion Daniel Mendoza. Known as "Mendoza the Jew," he had single-fistedly raised the community's social influence by being accepted by royalty and the social elite.

One "Son of Mendoza" who crossed through the ropes after Leach was Benny Leonard, known to his fans as "The Great Benny Leonard." Famed novelist Budd Schulberg remembers hearing his father, movie pioneer B. P. Schulberg, saying of their hero: "There was 'The Great Houdini.' 'The Great Caruso.' And 'The Great Benny Leonard.' That's how he was always referred to in our household," Schulberg wrote. But "The Great Benny Leonard" was neither "Great" nor "Leonard" in his youth. Truth to tell, his real name was Benjamin Leiner, and he grew up on New York's Lower East Side in a world where almost daily he was called upon to defend his Jewishness with his fists.

It was a world of hyphenated Americanism where street gangs were a way of life and youngsters of all persuasions not only staked out their so-called "territory," but fought to preserve it against outsiders. If it happened that some unlucky member of one gang strayed into another ethnic group's "territory," woe be to him as he had no choice but to fight his way out. Epithets like "Mick," "Kike," and "Wop" would fly as fast as sticks, stones, and fists, especially in the area which lay just beyond the street where

Leiner lived, an area designated by the city fathers as Eighth Street and Avenue C, but known locally as "No Man's Land."

Many of the free-for-all street skirmishes that were fought for supremacy and territory were ultimately decided by chosen representatives from each gang taking on each other in one-on-one set-tos. Although a scrawny lad of only 128 pounds, dripping wet, Leiner was almost always chosen as his gang's "designated hitter." And almost always he acquitted himself well in these head-on matches. One particularly grueling match took place against an Irish youngster named Joey Fogarty, a tough whose fists had become a permanent part of almost every Jewish kid's face in the neighborhood. Benny won the match and received the winner's share of sixty cents from the "gate" of one-cent admissions charged to members of both gangs. The 15-year-old Leiner soon decided to turn his talents into more, and larger, coin of the realm.

Adopting the name "Leonard"—after the famed minstrel performer of the time, Eddie Leonard, in the hope that Mama Leiner would not discover his new pursuit—Benny turned professional scant months after his brawl with Fogarty. His first fight was against one Mickey Finnegan for the princely sum of five dollars. Stopped in three rounds, Benny went home that night with nothing more than a bloody nose and the five dollars to show for his efforts. He was met at the door by his mother, who asked, in that disquieting way of mothers everywhere, "Where did you get this money?" Benny quietly answered, "By fighting, Mama." While his mother continued nattering on about how no son of hers would ever be a fighter, Benny's father sat staring at the five gold coins in his son's hand. Finally, Papa Leiner broke through the harangue to ask, "Benny, when will you fight again?"

And fight again Benny did, more than two hundred times over the next two decades. And in all but five of those fights—all five losses to Irishmen—Benny would rush to a telephone after the fight to call his beloved mother and tell her, "Hello, Ma. I won and I'm not hurt a bit." The busted beak fraternity took to calling him "Mama's Boy." But his devoted fans knew the man who ruled the lightweight division for seven long years as "The Great Benny Leonard."

Benny Leonard was but the first stone to hit the water, creating, in ever-widening circles, wave after wave of fighters from the ghettos of New York and elsewhere. In his wake came Maxie Rosenbloom, Al Singer, and Sid Terris from New York. Chicago spawned King Levinsky, Barney Ross, and Charlie White (born Charles Anchowitz), whose talents inspired Ernest Hemingway to pen the priceless line: "Life is the best left hooker I ever saw, although some say it was Charlie White of Chicago." There were Battling Levinsky, Lew Tendler, and Benny Bass from Philadelphia, and Jackie Fields (Jacob Finkelstein) from Los Angeles. And hundreds of ghetto battlers were also surfacing on the other side of the Big Pond, with first Ted "Kid" Lewis (Gershon Mendeloff) and then Jackie "Kid" Berg (Judah Bergman) carrying the banner for their adoring Jewish fans in London's Whitechapel. Berg would drive his followers literally "bonkers," as they say in Blighty, by climbing into the ring waving his tzitzis, or holy cloth, which he would proceed to hang on the ringpost as his battle flag.

Jewish fighters became so prevalent that Jewish fans would identify with anyone they thought was Jewish, much as their Irish brethren had decades before, cheering wildly for Max Baer, who wore a Star of David on his trunks but was not Jewish. (Not at least, according to longtime trainer Ray Arcel, who was asked to verify Baer's ethnic heritage. The old handler replied with relish, "He wasn't [Jewish]. I saw him in the shower.") And there was Sammy Mandell, who, in a manner similar to the fighters of a bygone era who had changed their names to appeal to Irish fans, shortened his name from Mandella to appeal to Jewish boxing fans in and around Chicago.

By the beginning of the thirties, the descendants of "Mendoza the Jew" so dominated the sport that boxing authority Joe Humphreys wrote: "The United States today is the greatest fistic nation in the world and a close examination of its four thousand or more fighters of note shows that the cream of the talent is Jewish."

By the 1930s the ring had become an extension of the street. And the street wars that had once been part and parcel of every inner city had now moved into the freelance world of the ring where matchmakers began to practice an early brand of "target marketing" long before Proctor & Gamble made it a standard practice. They structured their offerings to pit representatives of one ethnic group against those of another. Only now they were not fighting over turf, but for ethnic pride—and for the bragging rights that went with a win.

From these race war conditions three men emerged as emissaries of their respective ethnic groups, providing their fans with identification and rooting interest: Jimmy McLarnin, an Irishman; Barney Ross, a Jew; and Tony Canzoneri, an Italian.

Canzoneri—or "Canzi," the diminutive nickname adopted by adoring fans of the equally diminutive five-foot, four-inch boxer—was but the latest in a long line of great Italian fighters. Almost all before Canzoneri, however, had changed their surnames in order to enter boxing's mainstream. Thus a Peter Gulotta fought under the name Pete Herman, a Rocco Tozze as Rocky Kansas, a Rafelle Capablanca Giordano as Young Corbett III, and a Giuseppe Carrora as Johnny Dundee.

The story behind Johnny Dundee's name was one of the great boxing stories of the time. It seems that Dundee's manager,

Scotty Monteith, liked everything about his fighter except his name. "Carrora," Monteith would tell everyone who would listen, "sounded like carrots. Which made sense because his father used to run a market. I told him, 'If you fight with that name, they'll start throwing vegetables at you. You should take the name of my hometown in Scotland, Dundee.'" And so "Dundee" he became, the beloved "Scotch Wop." The name tripped easily over the tongue and was soon echoing through fight clubs large and small across the land, as his fans shouted for "Dun-dee . . . Dun-dee!" It also inspired other Italian fighters—Joe, Chris, and Angelo—to take the name of the Scottish town that Johnny had adopted.

Unlike those who had come before, Canzoneri came wrapped in the red, white, and green colors of his heritage, proudly bearing his family name. And he would bear the colors of his Italian fans proudly. But not immediately. With the build of a fireplug and the style of a house afire, Canzi built his career and his credentials by meeting and beating many of the day's top fighters in the lower weight divisions. Only nineteen when he won the featherweight crown from Benny Bass, Canzoneri knocked out Al Singer in the first round to win the lightweight championship in 1931, and Jackie "Kid" Berg in the third to claim the junior welterweight title the following year.

But, if popularity is glory's small change, even while Canzoneri was winning the glory, popularity eluded him. As it did in 1927 when he demolished the aging idol, Johnny Dundee. The cheers in Madison Square Garden that night were reserved for the fallen hero of Italian fight fans, Dundee, whose name it was that resounded from the rafters for almost an hour after the fight.

Four years later Canzoneri beat the dashing Cuban Kid Chocolate, but found himself again the target of small change, together with catcalls, jeers, cigar butts, and other miscellaneous flybys launched from the galleries of that psycho ward that was the old Garden. At a loss to explain his unpopularity, Canzoneri, choking back tears, could only say, "I don't know why they did that to me. I tried to make the fight and I won. . . . Some nights you just can't please 'em. . . ."

But it's a bad bargain that doesn't run two ways. And two years later Canzoneri was able to "please 'em," knocking the Cuban Bon Bon kicking in two rounds. For a full five minutes the gallery gods on the Forty-Ninth Street side of the Garden responded with an ear-splitting roar, stamping and calling for their new hero, Canzoneri. "Canzi" stood in mid-ring soaking up his newly-won adulation, saying over and over again, "I made them like me. . . . I made them like me. . . ."

After only eight years, Canzoneri was an instant success. And, in his newfound status as an authentic Italian hero, a real paisan, he fathered a new generation of Italian fighters, all born of the same hardscrabble homes and harder streets that earlier had bred Irish and Jewish fighters.

One of the most notable of the Italian stallions to follow Canzoneri's lead was Rocco Barbella, better known as Rocky Graziano. A favorite of the fight crowd from Sunnyside, Queens, all the way to Madison Square Garden, Graziano never lost the special rhythms and sounds of the New York streets. Time after time, in interviews peppered with "dese" and "dose," he said of his less than exemplary "yoot," "I never stole nuttin' unless it began with a 'A' . . . 'A truck' . . . 'A car' . . . 'A payroll.'" And, in a telling indication of just what the sport had meant to him, he would add, "If it wasn't for boxing, I woulda wounded up electrocuted at Sing Sing."

As Italian fighters took their place at the boxing table, the battles once fought on street corners for territorial rights now took place in the ring, ethnic undertones underlining almost every fight. Thus it was the Auld Sod versus the old tenement when a McLarnin took on a Leonard or an Al Singer or a Ruby Goldstein; or the old neighborhood versus the old ghetto when a Canzoneri met a Barney Ross or a Benny Bass or a Jackie "Kid" Berg. And each one of these mini-race wars lit up boxing's skies in an era before society was forced to conform to the latest fashion in political correctness.

But even as the sons of Erin, the sons of Mendoza, and the sons of Italy were fighting their way up the fistic ladder, there was something missing: the presence of black fighters, most of whom were toiling in relative obscurity or total invisibility, their fight for recognition thwarted by racial prejudice.

Such had not always been the case. Throughout boxing history, black fighters had been a part of the boxing scene. Their participation had begun early in the 1800s when ex-slaves Bill Richmond and Tom Molineaux left America to take on the reigning bareknuckle champions of Britain. Black participation continued throughout the nineteenth century and the first decade of the twentieth with the ascension of such great black fighters as Barbados Joe Walcott, George Dixon, and Joe Gans to world championships. But their titles were all in the lower weight classes, not in the heavyweight division, that being the special province of what white society called "The Strongest Man in the World." And specifically reserved for whites only.

The lone black heavyweight of note in the early days was the West Indian–born Peter Jackson. Unable to find opponents in his adopted land of Australia—he even offered to fight with his right hand "barred"—Jackson decided to try his luck in boxing's land o' plenty, America. His challenge was accepted by the outstanding contender for John L. Sullivan's title, James J. Corbett, with the assumption being that the winner would meet Sullivan for the championship. Although Corbett was a favorite of the California fight crowd, Jackson was the favorite among the "sports" who made him a 100–60 favorite to win. The bout took place on May 21, 1891, at San Francisco's California Club, the first in America ever conducted under the Marquess of Queensberry Rules, with gloves and three-minute rounds. It was one of boxing's all-time classics. Corbett would remember, "I soon discovered he was shifty and fast. And I thought I was fast!" After sixty-one evenly contested rounds, the referee approached both fighters and proposed that they call it "No Contest." Weary of the battle, both accepted.

Of course, Sullivan's impenetrable "Color Line" barred all men of color, so the title shot went instead to Corbett, who was pleased that he "would never have to face another sixty-one-rounder with Jackson again." The latter, according to his biographer David Wiggins, "developed a sadness and intimacy with misery" and partook of the camaraderie of newfound friends who lionized him in song and wined him in drink. This dual dissipation made a physical wreck of the once-great form that had been Peter Jackson. And although he was to fight a few more times, he was living on borrowed time. That time finally ran out on July 13, 1901, when he passed into, as it was then called, "the great majority." The official cause of death was listed as tuberculosis, although many believed that a broken heart contributed mightily to his demise. His epitaph sums up the man they called "The Black Prince" in just four words: "This was a man."

One man would prevail over boxing's caste system and that ineluctable verity which held that no black man could ever become the heavyweight champion of the world. That man was John Arthur Johnson. Known as "Li'l Artha," he was initially denied a chance to sink his roots in big-time boxing and forced to hone his skills against other black men on the so-called Chitlin' Circuit. With a victory over Sam Langford, his superior skills could no longer be denied and he began to menace white heavyweights much as Attila the Scourge of God had threatened the Romans. Dubbed "The Galveston Giant" by the press, he began taking on and quickly dispatching the likes of Joe Jeanette, Bob Fitzsimmons, and Jim Flynn. All that remained was the current champion, Tommy Burns, who chose to remain elusive. But Johnson was inevitability personified. He followed the champion to faraway Sydney, Australia where, after much pleading and even more wheeling and dealing, he got his long-awaited opportunity.

Fighting with an assurance that bespoke effrontery, Johnson soundly drubbed the champion on the day after Christmas, 1908. The victory unleashed a dammed-up wall of white hatred. But Johnson, whose natural ability was only rivaled by his contempt for the mores of white society, paid it no never mind. And, instead of practicing the obsequies and servilities expected of him, he marched across America disposing of brave plowboys, willing white women, and tall glasses of rum, all the while flaunting his color in the white man's face. The white man's "burden" had become its master.

Faced with this shocking, almost indigestible, challenge to Anglo-Saxon pride, writers like Jack London called for someone, anyone, to come forward to "remove that smile from Johnson's face" and avenge the defiling of the white Desdemona by this black Othello. A crusade was mounted to put the intruder in their midst back in his place, to remove this charge upon their honor.

Initially the crusade took the bloated form of former heavyweight champion Jim Jeffries, who was brought back to do battle with Johnson; a battle in the popular perception between the forces of good and evil. But the black man prevailed and the crusade failed. Momentarily. Next, a call went out for a "Great White Hope" to wrest the heavyweight crown from the infidel's hands and was answered by a ragtag lot of miners, cowpokes, gandy dancers, and lumberjacks. In 1915, a 265-pound former cowboy named Jess Willard came riding out of the West and, in twenty-six rounds under a hot Havana sun, removed that "smile" from Johnson's face and with it the threat to the Caucasian race.

(Johnson would make headlines one last time when, driving to New York to witness the second Joe Louis–Billy Conn fight in June of 1946, he lost control of his roadster near Raleigh, North Carolina, and died in the resulting crash. In one of sportswriting's immortal lines, John Lardner described it thusly: "Jack Johnson died crossing the white line for the last time.")

Dating from that day in 1915 when Johnson got his "due" until the early 1930s, the boxing establishment exacted revenge for the real and imagined slights of Johnson by turning its back on black fighters. In many cases promoters simply wouldn't promote a mixed bout, either due to prejudice or because a black fighter was not commercially saleable to the fight crowd, as it was then constituted. In others, many white fighters, invoking John L. Sullivan's sacred "Color Line," refused to fight blacks. And, in still others, some states outlawed fights between whites and blacks, not that the white fighter couldn't, or wouldn't—often by prearrangement—beat the black fighter, but the mere fact that a black man standing in the same ring with a white man conferred instant equality on the black man and white society couldn't have that. Whatever the method, the result was the same: the black boxer was relegated to the back of boxing's bus.

It was an era in which the heavyweight division was dominated by the commanding figure of Jack Dempsey, who wrested the title from Willard in 1919, knocking him down seven times in the first round. Dempsey was the perfect picture of the ring warrior. Approaching an opponent in his peculiar metronomic sway, teeth bared, black eyes flashing, and blue-black hair flying, the man the press called "The Man-Tiger" bore the look of an avenging angel. And any Dempsey opponent who could walk away from a fight considered it a success: some sixty foes, including those he met in exhibitions, failed to walk away from the first round. But Dempsey's place in boxing history cannot be measured by statistics alone. What Dempsey possessed, perhaps more than anyone ever on the landscape of American sport, was his ability to capture the imagination. Alone, he spawned what Paul Gallico called "The Golden Age of Sports" and was enshrined in the pantheon of 1920s greats long before Babe Ruth, Red Grange, Bill Tilden, or Bobby Jones. He was the greatest gate attraction of all time, without exception. The press coined the term "Million-Dollar Gate" solely to describe his many title defenses.

None of those title defenses, however, came against a black fighter. The "Color Line," dating back to John L. Sullivan, was invoked to prevent Dempsey from defending his title against a black contender. When the great Sam Langford, by then a half-blind old warrior in his third decade of boxing, came to Dempsey's manager, Doc Kearns, to beg for a chance to fight for the title, Kearns told him, "I'm sorry, Sam, we're looking for someone easier." And when Harry Wills, the universally accepted number one contender, signed to fight Dempsey, Tex Rickard, then the leading promoter, refused to stage the bout, citing the riots which had ensued after the last mixed match he had staged between Johnson and Jeffries. Furthermore, the New York State Athletic Commission and Governor Al Smith were opposed to mixed matches. And so Dempsey, feigning a headache or a similar infirmity, forfeited the $50,000 called for in the contract rather than face the man known as "The Brown Panther."

Al Reach, the publisher of *The Sporting News,* described the tenor of the times best when he chronicled the difficulties facing "Panama Joe" Gans, known as "The Black Secret." Reach wrote, "Jack Britton, the world's welterweight champion, was offered $20,000 to box Gans at Madison Square Garden; $25,000 was offered to Johnny Wilson, the present middleweight champion, but both champions decided to stay on the sunny side of the street and let this dark cloud roll by."

And so, with rare exceptions, black boxers were forced to sit on the curb as the parade passed them by. Some, like Tiger Flowers and the aforementioned Kid Chocolate, managed to break through the Caucasian curtain, but most were consigned to second-class citizenship, reduced to fighting each other, as Wills and Langford did a record twenty-two times. So good were many of them that one longtime observer called them "Black Murderers' Row." But regardless of their quality there still was no equality, no room at the boxing inn for them. Until 1934.

Nineteen thirty-three had seen the nation in the depths of the worst depression in its history. Not incidentally, it was also the worst of all years for the sport of boxing. Attendance and gate receipts hit an all-time low and the heavyweight champion, Primo Carnera, was a clown and a joke. If boxing had been a wake, it would have been an insult to the deceased. There was nowhere to go but up. In this darkest of times a white knight came to the rescue.

The white knight was, in reality, a black fighter out of Detroit. Christened Joseph Louis Barrow, his name had quickly been clipped by economy-minded ring announcers. National AAU light heavyweight champion in 1934, Louis had turned pro in

July of that year with a one-round knockout of an anonymity by the name of Jack Kracken. Louis registered eleven more wins that year, nine by KO, leaving his opponents with little physical capability save respiration. Word soon reached New York of Louis's exploits. Promoter Mike Jacobs negotiated a contract for exclusive rights to all of Louis's future bouts and put together a press party of twenty-five newsmen to see Louis fight in March of 1935, in Detroit. After an easy win over Natie Brown, their glowing reports about this unbeatable newcomer who had now won seventeen in a row, thirteen by KO, created a public demand for a look-see at the new heavyweight hope. That look-see came on June 25, 1935 in Yankee Stadium against the by-now ex-heavyweight champion Primo Carnera.

For twenty long years, from Jack Johnson to Joe Louis, no black fighter had ever stood on boxing's center stage. His victory was one for blacks everywhere. In her novel, *I Know Why the Caged Bird Sings,* Maya Angelou remembers what that evening of June 25, 1935 meant: "'[Carnera's] got Louis against the ropes,' said the announcer. . . . 'And it looks like Louis is going down.' My people groaned. It was our people falling. It was another lynching, yet another black man hanging on a tree. . . . It was hounds on the trail of a man running through slimy swamps. . . . It was a white woman slapping her maid for being forgetful. . . . We didn't breathe; we didn't hope; we waited. 'He's off the ropes, Ladies and Gentlemen!' shouted the announcer . . . 'Carnera is on the canvas. . . .' A black boy. Some black mother's son. He was the strongest man in the world."

Even while Louis ascended to the top of the heavyweight mountain, one he would ultimately scale by knocking out Jimmy Braddock for the title in 1937, another black fighter named Henry Armstrong was making a name for himself on the West

Coast. Armstrong had been a struggling featherweight, fighting in and around Los Angeles with mixed results against opponents as unknown as the soldier buried in Arlington National Cemetery. With Louis claiming more and more of the public attention, Armstrong felt he had to make a move. As he saw it, Louis was about "to take all the popularity, everything, away from me, away from all the fighters, because everyone was saving their money to see Joe Louis fight." Something had to be done before Armstrong—indeed all fighters, especially the black ones—were relegated to small Depression purses and even smaller agate newspaper type. Armstrong's Hollywood brain trust, Al Jolson and George Raft, came up with the "Big Idea": Armstrong would make ring history by going after three of boxing's eight divisional titles.

By the end of 1938, this perpetual motion machine had pulled off boxing's version of the "hat trick," winning the featherweight, lightweight, and welterweight titles—and holding them all simultaneously. Together, Louis and Armstrong became twin lighthouses, illuminating the path for other black fighters.

Still, it was Louis who was the main beacon. For no man was so admired and revered as this son of an Alabama sharecropper who carried his crown and himself with dignity and honesty. Using his words with the same commendable economy as he used his punches, Louis said a surprising number of things and said them in a way every American wished they had. There was his evaluation of his country's chances against the Axis powers in World War II: "We'll win 'cause we're on God's side." Dignity. And his enunciation of his opponent's chances in the second Billy Conn fight: "He can run, but he can't hide." Honesty. And with an obvious disinclination to repeat the mistakes of Jack Johnson in flaunting white society, Louis's manager, John Roxborough, laid down a harsh set of guidelines to regulate his conduct away from the ring:

1. He was never to have his picture taken alongside a white woman.

2. He was never to go into a nightclub alone.

3. There would be no soft fights.

4. There would be no fixed fights.

5. He was never to gloat over a fallen opponent.

6. He was to keep a "dead pan" in front of the cameras.

7. He was to live and fight clean.

Louis even eschewed being photographed eating one of his favorite treats, watermelon, lest it provide white society with ammunition to further stigmatize blacks.

When it was announced that Louis would defend his title against the German Max Schmeling in 1938, the event quickly became more than just a fight for boxing supremacy; it became a battle for supremacy between two warring ideologies. Inviting Louis to the White House, President Franklin Roosevelt tapped the champion on his massive, smithy-like arms and exhorted him to carry the standard for all Americans in democracy's war against totalitarianism, saying, "Joe, we're depending on those muscles for America."

Now the credentialed emissary of democracy, Louis already bore more than the twin burdens of heroism and patriotism on his shoulders as he climbed into the Yankee Stadium ring that night of June 22, 1938: the man in the other corner was the only one ever to have beaten him. But this time it wasn't much of a fight, more like a mugging belonging on page three rather than the sports page. Louis's murderous body punches bent Schmeling double and ferocious head shots reduced the representative of the so-called "Master Race" to resin. It took just two minutes and four seconds.

Joe Louis was a national hero. In the words of sportswriter Jimmy Cannon he was, "A credit to his race . . . the human race." And millions of Americans, black and white, now felt that way about the man most responsible—nine years before Jackie Robinson—for the democratization of American sports.

It would be nice to say that the process now repeated itself as thousands of black fighters followed the trail Louis—and to a lesser degree, Armstrong—had blazed, like their Irish, Jewish, and Italian predecessors. Nice, but untrue. For even though Louis and Armstrong had entered the white arena, the catalogue of black constituents still numbered just two. The rest of the black boxers were still being dealt to from the bottom of the deck, when they were dealt to at all. One who witnessed this discrimination first-hand was trainer Ray Arcel, who told interviewer Ronald Fried, with a sense of moral outrage, "The blacks of the '30s were the best fighters. There were no better fighters who ever lived than these fighters. They could do everything. They were in the gym waiting to substitute. But they never got work."

Most were resigned to their fate. But some, like "Tiger" Jack Fox, "Jersey" Joe Walcott, Elmer "Violent" Ray, "Snooks" Lacey, and "King Kong" Mathews, did find work, mostly at black fight clubs, like the Rockland Palace, Harlem's answer to Madison Square Garden. Still, according to fight publicist Irving Rudd, who worked The Palace: "There were two sets of unwritten rules, one for the fights between blacks and blacks and the other for fights between blacks and whites. It's not hard to figure . . . when a black guy goes up against 'one of his own kind,' the fight is a regular one, no deviations. But if a white guy is going against a black, the black fighter has to wear 'handcuffs' [take it easy], or do a tank job."

Even when black fighters did get work, they were still subjected to the indignities visited upon blacks in general by the white society of the time. Again, trainer Ray Arcel, who had a good heavyweight named Jimmy Bivins in Washington, D.C. for a fight in the early '40s: "The room they got him in a black hotel was a steambath," Arcel remembered. And so Arcel quickly approached a friend who managed a whites-only hotel where the trainer was staying. "I'm gonna ask you a favor," Arcel said to the manager. "I brought my valet with me." (The valet was, of course, Bivins.) "I got a room up there with two beds. Let him sleep up there, let him stay there." The manager answered, "Now listen to what I'm telling you. I'm gonna let you do it. But when you order his meals, you order for yourself. Don't let anybody see him. When they come up to take the dishes out, put him in the bathroom. No hanging out in the lobby. When he goes down that elevator . . . out, out the hotel. 'He made a delivery.' Know what I mean?" Arcel added, "And this was Washington, D.C., the capital of the United States!"

Even while black boxers were denied entry into the mainstream during the early '40s—their accomplishments standing out like labels on oceangoing steamer trunks—a seachange began taking place. Madison Square Garden, then the mecca of Boxing, seeking to refresh its pool of boxers, began bringing talented black fighters into the Garden for its regularly scheduled Friday night fights, fighters like Bob Montgomery, Ike Williams, Beau Jack, and the most exciting fighter yet, Sugar Ray Robinson.

These fighters, however, were in the lighter weight classes. The "big" breakthrough did not occur until December 5, 1947. "Jersey" Joe Walcott, who had been plying his trade in the backyards of boxing for almost two decades, was brought in to face heavyweight champion Joe Louis. Although Louis had defended his title twenty-three times before, Walcott was only his second black challenger. Surprisingly, the fight proved to be close, with the crowd-pleasing Walcott losing a controversial fifteen-round decision. Despite the loss, he won something less tangible but far more important: he opened doors to black boxers that had been closed to them since the time of Jack Johnson.

No longer treated like lepers, black fighters soon rose to the top in nearly every weight class: Archie Moore in the light heavyweights, Sugar Ray Robinson in the welterweights, Ike Williams in the lightweight division, and Sandy Saddler in the featherweight division, just to name a few, all using their fists to escape the lower rungs of society. In generations to come, the legacy of Louis would be carried on by others: Muhammad Ali, who would transcend the sport to become the symbol of his age, the turbulent '60s, much as John L. Sullivan and Jack Dempsey had reflected theirs; Marvelous Marvin Hagler, who refused to surrender to the streets and, through his fists, was able to retire with dignity and million-dollar trust funds for his children; and Mike Tyson, who was able to break the vicious grip of dependency, his children "being the first of my family members not on welfare." These African-American boxers, and many, many more, redeemed the down payment made by Louis sixty years before as boxing, to cop a time-worn phrase, finally, "regardless of race, creed or color," became "The Sport of Hope" for all.

Well, not all. Not yet, anyway. For there remained one group missing from boxing's group picture: the Hispanic or Latino fighter.

The first great American-born Latino fighter had been Manuel Ortiz, who ruled the bantamweight roost from 1943 to 1949, with one short two-month hiatus. But the list of other Latino fighters could be written on a postcard with a description of their neighborhoods on the other side and more than enough room left over for a return address, one that usually read "From Mexico" or "From Puerto Rico"—addresses early-day Latino boxing stars like Baby Arizmendi and Sixto Escobar called home.

The first trickle of American-born Latino fighters came in the 1950s as Art Aragon and Lulu Perez, among others, began to climb the fistic ladder. But it remained a trickle. One ascending the ladder was José Torres. A native of Ponce, Puerto Rico, Torres was a proud warrior and equally proud of his heritage. Before an early fight in the Bronx he grabbed the microphone and urged a noisy crowd of his compatriots to show pride. He asked them, "Did you know that Spanish was the first European language spoken in the western world? And that the first university in the new world was San Tomas Aquinas in Santo Domingo, the second San Marcos in Peru, and that ninety-nine years later the third was Harvard?" It was this kind of pride that fanned the sparks of self-esteem amongst Latino boxing fans.

Still, Latino fighters were as overlooked as Whistler's father. At least they were until the night of June 28, 1972. That night a quintessential warrior who gave new meaning to the Spanish word "machismo" burst upon the scene: Roberto Duran. That night he practically gelded Ken Buchanan to take the lightweight championship of the world. His victory heralded the advance of an army of Latino fighters who came tumbling out of the barrio to follow the banner of the man they called "The Hands of Stone."

It mattered little that Duran was a Panamanian, for this macho man gave heart to his American-born hermanos, a heightened sense of themselves. There was a sense of poetic justice to this, almost a reversal of Christopher Columbus pointing across the ocean and declaring, "There's a new world over there." Youngsters in the barrios who had had to scrap for everything now developed a strong appreciation of their Latino identity and marched—with a salsa or merengue beat—to the gyms.

The trickle rapidly swelled to a torrent as the likes of Bobby Chacon and Danny Lopez emerged. Soon it became a Niagara as Michael Carbajal, Johnny Tapia, Oscar De La Hoya, and hundreds of others stepped into the ring, all proudly bearing the mellifluous surnames that readily identified their Hispanic roots.

It was yet another variation on the time-honored theme: those on the lowest rung of society finding hope of a way out, a way out of a place where hope had always been a foreign language. With the emergence of the Latino fighters, boxing was truly an all-American sport, one which rang with the multicultural diversity of all of its ethnic groups.

II

Most of those from the tenements, the ghettos, the projects, and the barrios would never have succeeded in the ring, however, were it not for the trainer. No matter his background, the boxer was only one-half the equation, only one part of the story. The other was the trainer, whose emergence on the scene mirrored the pattern of the boxer, albeit a stutter-step behind.

In the early days, the trainer was little more than a "second," an aide whose function derived from dueling, the practice on which James Figg patterned boxing. As such, the trainer-second assisted the fighter in his preparation for the bout and acted as an intermediary in deciding the terms of the contest.

In time, one of the trainer's most essential functions emerged as he assumed the role of physical culturist. In one of the earliest tracts on the sport, *Fistiana*, Pierce Egan described the violent conditioning methods of the late eighteenth century:

> *The skillful trainer attends to the state of the bowels, the lungs, and the skin; and he uses such means as will reduce the fat, and, at the same time, invigorate the muscular fibres. The patient is purged by drastic medicines; he is sweated by walking under a load of clothes, and by living between feather-beds. His limbs are roughly rubbed. His diet is beef or mutton; his drink, strong ale; and he is gradually inured to exercise. . . . Beside his usual or regular exercise, a person under training ought to employ himself in the intervals in every kind of exertion, which tends to activity, such as cricket, bowling, throwing quoits, &c., so that, during the whole day, both body and mind may be constantly occupied.*

Over the next century this regimen would change little. Once again we must invoke the name of John L. Sullivan to provide a case in point. Having signed to defend his bareknuckle championship against Jake Kilrain, Sullivan immediately repaired to his favorite training grounds, the local saloons, there to spar more with bottles and broads than with barbells and bags. As the weeks leading up to the fight dwindled down to a precious few, and Sullivan began to resemble less the picture of a heavyweight champion than that of the dissolute wastrel, his frenzied manager, Billy Madden, prevailed upon the high priest of physical culture of the time, one William Muldoon, to take their battler in hand and end his slide into decadence.

Muldoon found Sullivan at one of his favorite watering holes doing battle with a stein of straight liquor. Called by his followers "The Noblest Roman of Them All," Muldoon was himself an awesome presence. He confronted the Heavyweight Champion of the World and, dashing his stein to the floor with one blow, physically dragged him out of the saloon and off to his health farm in western New York.

A firm believer that the extremes of the moment dictate their own rules, Muldoon instituted a carefully supervised program to reverse the effects of dissipation. As the first order of business, he banned all tobacco and alcohol. He substituted a regular dose of what he called "a first-rate purgative," a vile concoction made up of equal parts calcified magnesia, powdered rhubarb, and pulverized ginger.

Next, he dealt with the champion's bloated condition. In a staggering example of understatement, he referred to his charge as "a man who made flesh rapidly." Muldoon set out a clearly defined routine for the champion to turn that fat into muscle. At first, he put Sullivan to work alongside his farm hands, chopping down trees, plowing fields, even milking cows. A grumbling John L. would work with them, sweat with them, keep their hours, eat with them, and then gratefully collapse into bed at the same hour and in the same bunkhouse they did. Then gradually, as Sullivan's muscles began to harden and his wind improve, Muldoon moved him into working with the punching bags and a twelve-pound medicine ball. Soon the champion, who had been unable to manage even a few dozen rope skips, was doing eight hundred to nine hundred repetitions at a time. In less than eight weeks, Muldoon had performed miracles to rival those of Lourdes, transforming the tottering 240-pound hulk he had rescued from a saloon into a toddling 209-pound bear of a man, one who would reduce Jake Kilrain to plowshares in seventy-five hard-fought rounds.

Before this would happen, however, Muldoon had departed the scene. The miracle worker had had the inevitable falling out with his charge and was quickly replaced by the traditional "seconds" of the time, a ragtag band of hangers-on, water bucket carriers, and ex-fighters. Together they comprised a group of "trainers" assembled more to help the champion while away his time in camp than to aid in training. The champion was surrounded by the likes of manager Billy Madden, former heavyweight contender Joe Goss, buddies Pete McCoy and Bob Farrell, and his brother Mike, like Muldoon, Irishmen all.

The emergence of the modern-day trainer would have to await a new breed of boxer. And when that day dawned it would prove to be—as it had in Sullivan's day—a case of "like unto like," for the sport's new shining lights would be Jewish, as would their handlers.

Because history is, at best, imprecise, it is well-nigh impossible to identify the first Jewish trainer. Depending upon which yellowing newsclip one reads, it may well have been either Manny Seamon or Charley Goldman.

Goldman found his way into the corner through what would become the Ellis Island of all trainers: that of once having been a boxer. As a youth in the tough Red Hook district of Brooklyn, Goldman's start was the standard story, size seven. As he told author Ken Blady, "Little kids called you a 'Jew bastard,' so you punched them in the nose. I got to love it. Every time somebody called me a name, it meant I could have a fight without picking one."

Soon the young Goldman was hanging around with another neighborhood tough, Terry McGovern. But while "Terrible Terry" would go on to win the bantamweight and featherweight championships of the world, Goldman's career was far less illustrious, consisting of 137 documented fights, although Goldman put the number closer to three hundred. Often he fought for as little as five dollars in a private club or the back room of a saloon. The closest he ever came to matching McGovern came when he fought Johnny Coulon for the bantamweight championship in 1912, and when he adopted the signature derby hat of the great McGovern, an affectation that endured for the rest of his life.

By 1914, now a finished fighter in every sense of the word, the 26-year-old Goldman became a trainer. His first charge was Al McCoy. Born Alex Rudolph, McCoy, like so many other fighters of the time, adopted an Irish ring name to hide his profession from his Orthodox Jewish parents. McCoy was an obscure fighter who got a shot at the middleweight title through what can only be described as a "fluke." He had signed to fight Joe Chip. But when Chip fell ill on the eve of the fight, his brother, George—not incidentally, the middleweight champion—was brought in as a replacement to save the payday. In those days of "no decision" fights, the title could only change hands by a knockout, and the out-of-shape middleweight champion, the victim of a knockout just once in seventy-five fights, took the light-hitting McCoy lightly.

Too lightly, it turned out. Goldman told his charge to "go in with a right-hand lead as soon as it starts and, when his guard comes up, hit him in the belly with everything you've got!" McCoy did. And did. And the champion went down like a balloon with the string removed, air escaping, in just forty-five seconds of the first round.

Goldman's gnarled hands would work many other corners, including those of champions Lou Ambers, Marty Servo, and Joey Archibald. The cornerstone of his fame, however, rested on his molding Rocky Marciano into one of the all-time greats.

The first time Goldman laid eyes on Marciano, then just Rocco Marchegiano, he had hitched a ride on the back of a vegetable truck from his Brockton, Massachusetts home to see the trainer. As Marciano disembarked, Goldman, so the story goes, took one look at the green goods and said, "You look worse than the cabbages." Goldman took Marciano in hand, studying his style—or lack thereof—the way a biologist does a specimen. What he observed was one of boxing's irregularities. As he told it, "Marciano was so awkward we just stood there and laughed. He didn't stand right, he didn't throw a punch right . . . he threw them from his behind. He didn't do anything!" And so the master alchemist went to work, teaching his charge the rudiments of boxing: the jab, the hook, footwork, the barest bones of the sport. The one thing Goldman wouldn't touch was Marciano's powerful right hand, which he dubbed the "Suzie Q." It was boxing's version of Pygmalion and Galatea as Goldman turned the piece of rock into a polished fighter named Rocky Marciano.

But even though Goldman could lay claim to having been one of the great trainers of all time, his claim to having been the first Jewish trainer is subject to dispute. The other candidate for that honor is Manny Seamon, who, at the tender age of 16, his face still a stranger to the razor, began his career "rubbing Leach," referring to the celebrated Jewish fighter Leach Cross. In another case of like-unto-like, Seamon also trained Benny Leonard and Ted "Kid" Lewis, two more Jewish greats. The crowning moment of his career, however, came when he took over as trainer for Joe Louis after Jack Blackburn's death in 1942.

Goldman and Seamon were but the first ripples in the stream. They were followed by wave upon wave of other Jewish trainers. And by the beginning of the thirties, just as the Jewish fighter had risen to the top, so too had the Jewish trainer. Two prominent examples were Ray Arcel and Whitey Bimstein, a duo fittingly called "The Siamese Training Twins." The 1930 *Everlast Boxing Record Book* wrote of the two:

> *Trainers capable of acting as most capable seconds to a fighter in actual combat are as rare as an eclipse of the sun. Two young men, regarded as the leading exponents of the training and seconding are men who are giving their older conferees a close contest for honors, Ray Arcel and Whitey Bimstein, the Siamese Twins. The responsibility boils itself down to Arcel and Bimstein, who are given complete control of the boxer. Most managers, in fact, leave the seconding of their battler entirely in the hands of this duet, their methods having been successful.*

Arcel would "train and second" such fighters as Charley Phil Rosenberg, Benny Leonard, Jackie "Kid" Berg, James J. Braddock, Ezzard Charles, and almost all of Joe Louis's opponents—so many, in fact, that he was known as "The Meat Wagon." One of his duties as handler of the Louis challengers included carting away their remains after they had been decimated by "The Brown Bomber."

Bimstein, who broke in seconding the great Harry Greb, was known as "The Surgeon" and is best remembered in the broken-beak biz for his surgical work in Rocky Graziano's corner during "Da Rock's" second fight with Tony Zale, "The Man of Steel." The fight, more savage than scientific, had been a seesaw battle.

But, by the end of the third round, Graziano was by far the worse for wear, his right eye bleeding and swollen, stumbling around the ring blindly. As Graziano returned after the third round he screamed, "Get my eye open!" Bimstein spent the entire sixty-second intermission between the third and fourth rounds working on the damaged eye and arguing with the referee, who wanted to stop the fight. While applying pressure to the eye with a silver dollar in an effort to restore vision, Bimstein pleaded, "Give Rocky one more round!" According to Graziano, referee Johnny Behr responded, "If this wasn't a championship fight, I would never have let him last out the third round. One more, and if he don't come out of it, I got to stop it. . . . They give you the chair for murder in this state." With sight restored in the damaged eye, Graziano turned the fight around, knocking his opponent out in the sixth to win the middleweight championship. After the fight, in an ending tailor-made for Hollywood, a battered and beaten Graziano took the microphone and screamed at the crowd, "Ma, I told ya. . . . Your bad boy done it. . . . Somebody up there likes me!"

And then, just as Jewish trainers had followed Jewish boxers, Italian trainers now followed their Jewish counterparts into the corners.

The first of the famous Italian trainers was Al Silvani, who had been initiated into the brotherhood of trainers by Whitey Bimstein in 1936. Later he had worked with Ray Arcel after the two "Siamese Twins" had separated. In another like-unto-like scenario, Silvani then went off on his own to train heavyweight contender Tami Mauriello and later teamed with Bimstein to train Rocky Graziano.

However, Silvani's favorite story had nothing to do with Mauriello—whom he navigated into a title fight against Joe Louis—or Graziano. It involved a skinny Italian boy, then 119 pounds dripping wet, who once asked Silvani to train him in the finer points of "The Sweet Science." It was Frank Sinatra. As a favor, Silvani approached the Garden's powers-that-be and asked if they would let Sinatra sing the National Anthem before Mauriello's fight against Jimmy Bivins in March of 1943. Their initial response was, "This fight is going on coast-to-coast radio and we can't have an unknown singing the Star Spangled Banner." They later relented and Sinatra got his first national exposure. Unfortunately, he did better than Silvani's other protege, Mauriello, who lost a ten-rounder to Bivins.

Soon, other Italian trainers followed the path blazed by Silvani into boxing's corners. There were the Florio Brothers, Nick and Dan. And Chickie Ferrara. And the man Ferrara handed his arcane knowledge down to, like a family heirloom, Angelo Dundee. The latter had changed his family name, Mirena, to that traditional Italian fight name Dundee. And, in keeping with another boxing tradition—that of "like unto like"—his first champion would be a fellow paisan, Carmen Basilio. And then there was boxing's master psychologist, Cus D'Amato. And Lou Duva and Joey Fariello. And hundreds of others, all leaving their mark on boxing's long and rich history.

Conspicuously absent were black faces. Their presence in corners had mainly been a rumor, unreported in "the white man's papers" except as "bottle washers." One small mention appeared in a London newspaper of 1810 of a black "second" in the corner of Tom Molineaux, the ex-slave who had come to England to challenge Tom Cribb for the heavyweight crown. That "second" was Bill Richmond, known as "The Black Terror" during his fighting days. According to the account, Richmond, the son of a Georgia slave, had "raised his mauleys" to challenge the same Cribb five years earlier.

It would be another century-plus before Jack Blackburn followed Richmond as a trainer in a big fight. Blackburn was a lightweight who had taken on all comers during the first two decades of the twentieth century, including the great Sam Langford. Many times Joe Louis would say, "They fought more draws than a man draws breath." After hanging up his gloves, Blackburn turned his considerable boxing "smarts" to the training of fighters—mostly white fighters.

One day in 1934, Blackburn was in a Chicago gym when he was approached by John Roxborough, a Detroit numbers operator. Roxborough wanted him to handle his new heavyweight. When Blackburn told Roxborough to bring around his "white boy and I'll look him over," he was informed that his "boy was black." Skeptical of the opportunities available to a black heavyweight, Blackburn shook his head and said, "I'll have no truck with a colored boy . . . colored boys ain't got much chance fighting nowadays unless they happen to be world-beaters." Roxborough laughed and said that's exactly what he had. And what he had was Joe Louis.

But Blackburn was singularly unimpressed by his first look at Louis. In a 1937 interview in *The Ring Magazine* Blackburn said:

When Roxborough brought Louis to me, he was just a big, easy-going Negro boy with high water pants and too much arms for his coat sleeves. "So you think you can go somewhere in this fighting game?" I said to him, "Well, let me tell you something right off. . . . It's next to impossible for a Negro heavyweight to get anywhere. He's got to be very good outside the ring and very bad inside the ring. Mr. Roxborough, who has known you quite a while, is convinced you can be depended on to behave yourself. But you've got to be a killer, otherwise I'm too old to waste any time on you."

To which Louis replied, "I ain't gonna waste any of your time." Louis wouldn't. A willing student, he quickly absorbed everything Blackburn tried to impart to make him a complete fighter: balance, how to deliver a good left jab, and how to step in while throwing a punch. In short time Louis was disposing of his opponents with a dismal monotony and startling variety. And the firm of Louis & Blackburn began to assume epic proportions.

Inspired by Blackburn's success, the Fates, trying to balance the ledger, shifted their attention to black trainers, somewhat in arrearages. Soon they were filling corners and speaking "soul to soul" with their black charges, trainers like Eddie Futch, Georgie Benton, Manny Steward, and hundreds of others.

It was the same with Latino trainers as the Victor Vallees and Edwin Viruets soon crouched in the corners of Latino fighters, speaking to them the language of the ring in their native tongue.

And by the final decade of the twentieth century, the trainer had become more than merely a party of the second part; he had by now become part of the whole. Part of the equation.

The pairing of a youngster with a caring trainer is all important, for the trainer becomes a surrogate father, a father confessor, a mentor to a young man who may never have known his father.

How does a fighter choose a trainer? One London trainer, Harry Giver, once said, "I've lost count of the number of boys who have been referred to me by the local probation officers. I persuaded them that it was better to see their names in the sports pages of the local newspaper than the court reports, and in return I got absolute loyalty from them."

Most trainers "adopt" their charges not because, as Charley Goldman, Rocky Marciano's trainer, put it, "Training promising kids is like putting a quarter in one pocket and taking a dollar out of another." They do it because they care for them and it often becomes a mutual relationship. Despite his seemingly callous remark, Charley Goldman is said to have died of a heart attack in his room in training camp covered with one of Rocky's old robes.

The tales of a trainer's caring nature surface time and again. As former fighter Danny Kapilow told interviewer Ronald Fried, "Ray Arcel's greatest asset was his care . . . caring for you as an individual, as a person, beyond the fact that you might earn some money for him." That "care" manifested itself in many ways. "Pop" Foster trained and managed Jimmy McLarnin for his entire career and, when he passed away, he left his entire estate to his foster son, McLarnin, including a handsome parcel of real estate in downtown Los Angeles. When Joe Frazier got up off his stool for the fifteenth round of "The Thrilla in Manilla," his trainer, compassionate Eddie Futch, told him, "Sit down, son. It's all over. No one will ever forget what you did here today."

As Angelo Dundee, the trainer of Muhammad Ali and Sugar Ray Leonard, puts it, for the combination of fighter and trainer to be successful, "You got to blend yourself to the fighter." That blending consists of equal parts of being physician, baby-sitter, and psychologist, garnished with more than a healthy dose of caring.

Jack Blackburn was part psychologist when he told Joe Louis, before his fight with Buddy Baer, "Don't let this last too long because there's a good show up at the Apollo Theater later. Let's get up there." Then there was Whitey Bimstein. Described by journalist Hal Conrad as looking "like a clown without make-up," Whitey was never pictured in a fighter's corner without a Q-tip tucked behind his ear. One of his fighters, Vinnie Ferguson, characterized him as "one of the best psychologists in the world. He would light a fire under you. . . . He'd maybe tell you that the other guy insulted you. . . . He'd say, 'This guy can't carry your jockstrap' or 'This guy is a baby compared to you. . . .'"

One of the best stories about Bimstein as an amateur shrink comes from Fred Apostoli's 1940 match with Melio Bettina. Apostoli returned to his corner after taking a beating and asked, "What's the matter with me? I can't fight!" The trainer didn't say a thing, he just hauled off and hit his fighter in the face and hollered, "Now get out there and do your stuff." Apostoli went out in the next round and beat the bejabbers out of Bettina. When he returned to his corner he said to Bimstein, "That's what I needed. Sock me again, but hard! Get me mad!"

Most fighters are, like Apostoli, grateful recipients of the trainer's contributions to their success. Muhammad Ali said of Angelo Dundee, "After Frazier beat me, after Spinks beat me, he made me believe again. Angelo really had more confidence in me than I did."

As Ali, Louis, Marciano, and every other fighter who ever laced up his gloves knows, the trainer is the one element essential to ultimate success. And the care extended by their trainers is reciprocated by almost all who credit their managers with having taught them the proverbial "ropes"—in boxing and in life.

Ultimately though, every boxer is alone in the ring, naked but for his silk trunks, armed only with his fists and his wits, seeking to outbox, outwit, outlast his opponent. As Buster Mathis Sr. once said of his manager and trainer when they had used the pluralistic "we" once too often, "Where do they get that 'we' shit? When the bell rings, they go down the steps and I go out in the ring alone." It is a hard way of life. But boxing has never sought its enlistees from the debutante line at the local country club. Instead, it recruits them from the crucible of the streets, boy-men who have fought their way out of the slums, the ghettos, the projects, the barrios, the "nabes," expressing themselves the only way they could . . . with their fists in "The Sport of Hope."

AMERICA FINDS A HERO: JOHN L. SULLIVAN

John Lawrence Sullivan. The very name brings back memories to that rapidly dwindling number of fight fans whose fathers saw this bull-like man club opponents into the earth with an awesome right and told them about his exploits. To the average adult, he is a storied figure in boxing history who gave color to his age, somewhat in the fashion Babe Ruth and P. T. Barnum gave color to theirs. To the younger generation, he is merely a name, spoken in reverential terms by elders and used as a benchmark for modern boxers like Joe Louis and Muhammad Ali.

In a time when national heroes have passed from the American landscape, it is difficult to fathom Sullivan's full impact. People who couldn't care less about boxing knew his name. But John L. Sullivan was more than a name—he was an institution, a deity. He was called "the Boston Strongboy," "Spartacus Sullivan," "Knight of the Fives," "Sullivan the Great," "His Fistic Highness," "Prizefighting Caesar," "the Hercules of the Ring," "the Youthful Prince of Pugilists," "America's Invincible Champion," and hundreds of other names meant to convey just one thing: that he was the idol of American youth and the symbol of boxing the world over.

As each day brought new accolades and exaggerated stories about the man who had become a legend in his own time, Sullivan contributed to the lore by writing and then rewriting the record books with every swing of his mighty fists. "My name is John L. Sullivan and I can lick any sonofabitch in the house," he would roar with a swaggering virility that mirrored the times, times when America was confident and cocksure, already convinced of its place in history but still casting about for its true identity. And John L. Sullivan gave it both history and identity.

His popularity transcended pugilism, transporting every red-blooded American into a hero worship not seen before or since. It gave rise to the pet slogan of the 1890s, "Let me shake the hand that shook the hand of The Great John L.," a line strong enough to open the popular Broadway play *A Rag Baby*, and a line strong enough to carry the feelings of a country imbued with its own strength—and the strength of a man who epitomized America the world over.

Born in Boston of Irish immigrant parents on October 15, 1858, the baby christened John Lawrence was a sturdy and feisty babe at birth, inheriting his size from his mother—a big-boned woman who weighed almost 180 pounds—and his fighting temperament from his father, a five-foot-three street scrapper.

Apparently feeling that one fighter in a family was more than the neighborhood quota, Mrs. Sullivan directed her son toward the priesthood. But young John L. was, at best, whelmed with the idea, and after what he claimed later to be sixteen months of study at an institution that has since become Boston College, left and apprenticed himself first to a plumber and then to a tinsmith. He was dismissed from both jobs for fighting.

Sullivan, in his autobiography, was to admit to being capable of handling his dukes. "I had many a fracas with the other fellows," he was to write, adding, as if there was any doubt, "And I always came out on top."

This young giant, who was well on his way to the top, took a minor detour to indulge himself in yet another American passion—baseball. By 1886 *Harper's Weekly* heralded the coming of baseball, even then being called "the Nation's Pastime" by saying, "The fascination of the game has seized upon the American people, irrespective of age, sex or other condition." And one man who was in condition, young John L., seized upon the game to exhibit his athletic abilities, which were so great that not only was he paid $25 a game by the semipro team with which he played, but he boasted he had earned an offer from the manager of the Cincinnati Reds for $1,300 a season.

But John L. turned down the offer in order to concentrate on his growing passion, pugilism. It had all begun one night when a touring tough at a boxing exhibition announced he would take on any man in the house and offered any and all comers the then unheard-of amount of $50 if they could but stay three rounds. Almost immediately the chant of "Sull-i-van, Sull-i-van" permeated the theater as they called upon their local hero to take on the stage fighter and make him eat his words.

John L. removed his coat and strode mightily onto the stage, there to put on boxing gloves for the first time in his life. As he reached out to shake hands, he received a punch in the nose for his efforts. Angered by the affront, Sullivan roared into the perpetrator of this foul act and knocked him senseless, head-over-challenge into the orchestra pit.

Soon John L. was fighting professionally, beating the local scrappers, including the man known as the heavyweight champion of Massachusetts. After going on an exhibition tour himself, offering each and every comer $50 if they stayed four rounds—few of whom dared and none of whom did—he got the opportunity to fight Professor Mike Donovan, then-world middleweight champion, in a three-round exhibition. As Sullivan would later relate the tale of his fight with one of the first great scientific boxers in America, "it was my first chance to become famous." And it was a chance he wasn't about to let slip by. "All Boston assembled to witness my slaughter, but I surprised them and my opponent, too, by standing him off." The reputation of the Boston Strongboy grew more than a little bit as he battered the Professor and all but knocked him out.

"After our bout, when we had reached our dressing rooms upstairs, we had a long talk. 'John,' Donovan said, 'I really believe you tried hard to knock me out.' 'Oh no,'" Sullivan claims he replied, and winked at one of his seconds, "I didn't try very hard to finish you." Donovan, according to Sullivan, replied, "Well, I'm going to be honest with you, John, and tell you that I tried my best to knock you out, and I was surprised when I failed."

Sullivan, perhaps embellishing the story but making a good tale in the telling, replied in kind to Donovan, or so he claimed, "Well, I'll also be honest, and tell you that I came within an inch of putting the knockout wallop over. If you hadn't dodged that last one that was aimed at your jaw, you wouldn't have come to yet."

Of such stuff are legends made. And if the fight itself wasn't enough, when Donovan returned to New York he told everyone and anyone who would listen that he had found a comer up in Boston who would soon take the measure of anyone he fought. Among the interested parties listening to Professor Donovan's stories were Joe Goss, the American champion, and George Rooke, claimant to the middleweight champion.

Rooke's comments are unrecorded, but Goss is reputed to have said something like, "Oh, tell that to the sailors," or whatever passed for "applesauce" in those days, and implored Donovan to set something up so, "I can get a peep at him."

William Muldoon and Billy Madden, Sullivan's manager, arranged for Goss to take such a "peep" at Sully at a Boston testimonial for Goss on April 6, 1880. It was an opportunity for Sullivan, one that he later claimed, "Gave me my first chance to demonstrate to the wise ones that I was going to become one of the world's greatest exponents of the manly art of fighting," or so one of his ghostwriters, acting as a dishonest ventriloquist, would put in his memoirs.

The three-round sparring exhibition had hardly started when Goss got his first "peep," a hard right to the chin. In the second the two were slugging toe-to-toe when suddenly Sully, in his own words, "Let loose a right-handed swing and knocked him flat." Goss was dragged to his corner and revived by his seconds. As the two men advanced for the beginning of the third, two of Sullivan's friends advised him to carry the old champ. He did, sparring through the last round and not trying for a knockout. Even so, Goss had become a believer, turning to the referee as he left the ring and confiding, "That fellow's blows feel like the kick of a mule."

The next day the local papers, which barely carried two inches on an important fight or fighter, dedicated an article to Sullivan and his punching power, proclaiming "Sullivan's terrific hitting on this occasion proved quite a sensation." It was the start of the legend of John L.

But the legend of John L. extended only so far—Boston and environs. In order to further his fame and fortune, Sullivan went on a road trip, doing the vaudeville circuit, again taking on all comers.

Sullivan's notoriety would rest on three fights he would have the year after reaching his majority. The first of these was against veteran George Rooke, the self-proclaimed middleweight champion, whom he took out in two rounds. Next stop, Cincinnati, where his manager, Billy Madden, challenged "the Champion of the West," Professor John Donaldson. Madden was famous for advertising his charge by challenging every heavyweight in sight. If the man challenged failed to respond, and quickly, Madden usually laid claim to the delinquent pugilist's title, if he were champion, and promptly announced that his man was ready to defend the newly acquired honor against all comers.

Donaldson chose not to duck the challenge. Instead he saved his ducking, sidestepping, and sprinting for the fight itself, a fight that could have been refereed by Lon Myers, an early-day Jesse Owens, who had just won the national 100-, 220-, 440-, and 880-yard titles. Donaldson clinched and frequently dropped to the ground without taking a punch, thus ending a round under the old London Prize Fight Rules. The frustrated Sullivan finally caught up with his unworthy adversary in the tenth, laying him endwise.

Notwithstanding the fact that the so-called "fight" was one in name only, the local constabulary arrested Sullivan and charged him with participating in an "illegal" prizefight. Brought before a judge on the charge, Sullivan was vindicated when one witness described the so-called match as a "foot race," and went on to say, "Donaldson is a fine sprinter. He was mostly in the lead by a quarter of a mile, but Sullivan was hot on his trail. . . . Then he barely touched him, just to let him know he had caught up. . . . That was the finish. Donaldson was tripped up and couldn't continue."

The charges were dismissed. But what couldn't be dismissed was Sullivan's reputation. And ambition. The next day he issued an any-man-in-the-house challenge to a match, publishing an ad in the *Cincinnati Enquirer* that read:

> *I am prepared to make a match to fight any man breathing, for any sum from one-thousand dollars to ten-thousand dollars at match weights. This challenge is especially directed to Paddy Ryan and will remain open for a month if he should see fit to accept it.*
>
> *Respectfully yours,*
> *John L. Sullivan*

But heavyweight champ Paddy Ryan would have none of John L., or his braggadocio, and hid behind a public dismissal of the challenge which read, "Go and get a reputation," but which might have sounded more like "Go fly a kite." Sullivan was not deterred, and he went out in search of that reputation, heading toward the city where reputations are often built taller than buildings: New York.

The man Sullivan and Madden selected already had a mighty reputation of his own. Around and about New York, the name John Flood was bigger than that of John L. Sullivan. A well-connected man with Tammany Hall and a well-proportioned pugilist, the man known as the "Bull's Head Terror" had won considerable fame bowling over anyone put in front of him. Possessing a powerful physique built on a six-foot-two-inch frame, Flood had never failed to "get his man" and was considered, at least by New Yorkers, more than a match for Sullivan, and his superior in every way.

At the time of the Sullivan–Flood fight there were stringent laws in New York—as there were throughout the country—against both boxing and prizefighting. The managers of Sullivan and Flood finally decided to hold the fight aboard a barge to circumvent any possible interference by the local upholders of law and order.

And so it was on the night of Monday, May 16, 1881, that the heroes of the two great Eastern metropolises fought for personal pride, reputation, and $1,000 on a barge moored off Yonkers, New York, with kid gloves and under London Prize Ring Rules. Within 16 minutes Sullivan had battered Flood to the wooden floor three times. Suddenly a shout rose above the crowd. "There's a police boat coming."

Sullivan redoubled his efforts and Flood's seconds mercifully threw in the towel indicating their charge's surrender. "We met as friends and we part as friends," Sullivan was heard to say to his opponent as he went over to shake the fallen hulk's hand. Then, espying Paddy Ryan in the crowd, he shouted, "You'll be the next one." Ryan yelled back, "You'll get your chance yet."

Sullivan would, but it would take the intercession of one of the most powerful men in the United States, Richard K. Fox, publisher of the *Police Gazette,* to get the two parties together— and then, only under the banner of his publication for promotional purposes and personal prestige.

When Richard Kyle Fox, a penniless 29-year-old immigrant, came to the United States in 1874, he found work on a New York newspaper. The bounds of his ambition had hardly been tapped, though. With the few hundred dollars he had saved and a few more that he borrowed, Fox bought the *National Police Gazette.*

Infusing it with a dose of promotional savvy, he was able to revive the moribund publication. Part of the rebirth experience included the addition of a new masthead that read "Richard K. Fox, Editor and Proprietor," and the creation of a sports section, bringing accounts of prizefights and races to the general public. The sports page was a novelty and the ten-cent weekly soon earned Fox a considerable reputation among Americans who were eager for such coverage.

Prizefighting was illegal in every one of the thirty-eight states in 1880, but Fox followed his intuition, assigning a group of artists and reporters to cover the championship match between England's Joe Goss and Paddy Ryan, an American, at Collier Station on the Virginia-Pennsylvania border.

The battle over, a special edition of the *Gazette* was issued. Complete with artist's renderings of the fight and a detailed description of the match, the presses rolled on relentlessly until the magazine answered the sport-thirsty public's demand. As the *Police Gazette* poured into every barbershop, pool hall, saloon, police station, fire hall, and major male gathering-place in the country, Fox knew he had created a journalistic sensation.

His fame, however, issued from yet another occurrence. Due to a slight suffered at the hands of John L. Sullivan, Fox would soon set the course for boxing in America. Spurred by his enormous ego, Fox would become our first boxing promoter. Unofficially, of course.

Harry Hill's Dance Hall and Boxing Emporium, a group of two-story buildings on Houston Street in New York, offered wrestling and boxing exhibitions as a divertissement for the stage and sports personalities of the time who made it their second home: P. T. Barnum, Diamond Jim Brady, Lillian Russell, James Gordon Bennett, and also Richard K. Fox, the most influential sports figure in America. It was to Harry Hill's that Sully went during a brief visit to New York.

A foolhardy challenger from the audience had just added his name to Sullivan's injured warrior list. The $50 won by Sullivan remained liquid as he reinvested it in drinks for his admirers, his friends and various hangers-on.

Suddenly, a waiter appeared next to Sullivan with the message, "Mr. Fox would like a word with you."

The answer, bellowed to the waiter, was heard by everyone in the establishment.

"You tell Fox that if he's got anything to say to me he can Gahdamn well come over to my table and say it!"

Fox, never having been addressed in such a manner, was loath to forget the affront. He certainly never forgave it.

Soon Fox began an intense search for a boxer who could "get" Sullivan. In Paddy Ryan he found his man.

Ryan, the holder of the belt, had kept it and the title for a little over a year, but showed no proclivity for risking it in the ring, especially against so formidable an opponent as the Boston Strongboy. Finally, with Fox as his backer and operating as the de facto promoter, Ryan agreed to the bout, $5,000 a side. But here a hitch developed. After $500 of the stake money was deposited with Harry Hill in New York, Sullivan's backers had difficulty coming up with the remainder of the $5,000. It was Ryan who saved the bout by appealing to Fox to reduce the stakes by half because of Sullivan's inability to obtain sufficient funds.

The reluctance of Sullivan money was rooted in the unsettled state of boxing at that time in the United States. While most fights were then fought under the old London Prize Ring Rules—bare knuckles and rounds ending when a man was knocked, tripped, or thrown to the ground and having thirty seconds to come "to scratch"—Sullivan was an ardent advocate of the new Marquess of Queensberry Rules.

In fact, Sully had begun a crusade against the use of bare fists in his travels around the country and had started to popularize the use of gloves, called "pillows" by their detractors. While Ryan had established himself as a bareknuckle fighter, Sullivan's ability as one was practically unknown. Stimulated by the relative merits of both fighters, talk of the match filled the land—and, not incidentally, the *Police Gazette*.

Sullivan was then a 24-year-old Adonis, a perfect athlete who, up until this point in his career, had abstained from all forms of tobacco and strong drink, in radical contrast to his later habits. And so, with workouts more of a nicety than a necessity, each person in Sullivan's Mississippi training camp became dedicated to this man and his winning of the crown, but not overly concerned with their warrior's condition or chances.

His camp's somewhat relaxed atmosphere produced one of those little sidebars that illumines boxing's history—one that has totally escaped notice. During a break in the regimen, Madden, trainer Pete McCoy, and second Mike Gillespie were out in the fields kicking a football—or more accurately, a soccer ball—around when the idea suddenly occurred to McCoy that a football hung from the ceiling would improve his charge's proficiency at hitting a moving target. And, from that day on, the punching bag became an important adjunct to every fighter's training program.

The Sullivan–Ryan fight itself was anticlimactic. On the morning of February 7, 1882, Sullivan and Ryan met in a ring pitched in front of the veranda of the Barnes Hotel in the Gulf resort town of Mississippi City, Mississippi. The two men approached the ring and threw their hats into it, indicating they were ready for combat.

Almost immediately the Troy Giant rushed Sullivan with the intention of battering down the defenses of the 100–80 favorite. But Sullivan held his ground and gave back everything with interest, ending the first round by smashing Ryan to the ground with one of his thunderous rights—a right Ryan would later recall as feeling like "a telephone pole had been shoved against me endways." Round 2 saw Ryan come back and throw Sully heavily to the ground, ending the round. That was Ryan's last hurrah. As Sullivan took charge in the third round, throwing fearful punches with either hand, a frustrated Fox screamed vainly to Ryan to inflict damage on his sworn enemy. Finally, after nine rounds, taking ten minutes and thirty seconds, Sullivan caught Ryan with a fearful right and knocked him senseless. Fox was incensed.

Taking one look at his fallen opponent, the new American heavyweight champion vaulted the ropes and sprinted to his quarters, all the quicker to start the postprandial party scheduled for the train trip back to New Orleans.

After some prodigious partying in the Crescent City, the once-abstemious champion went home to a rousing reception. Back in Back Bay the new champion reportedly put on a drinking exhibition seldom seen before, even in Boston. High living and heavy drinking soon became Sullivan trademarks, adding a new dimension to the character of America's new hero, that of the arrogant swashbuckler who could fight or drink two-handed. Both very well, thank you!

The newly crowned American champion immediately set out to merchandise himself, barnstorming across the country on a knockout trip that made boxing popular and John L. well-to-do. The going price was now $1,000 for anyone who could last four rounds with the heavyweight champion under Queensberry Rules. Boasting, "I can beat any sonofabitch in the house," he would totter out nightly to center stage so drunk that his handlers had to help him into his tights and push him in the direction of the curtain. But he was able to back-up his defiance by meeting and beating a collection of local barkeeps, bullyboys, and blacksmiths, with an occasional "professional" fighter thrown in for good measure.

The only one of the hundreds of challengers who stayed the course was an experienced British heavyweight, Joe Wilson. Fighting under the name "Tug" Collins, he was backed by none other than Sullivan's adversary, Richard K. Fox. Persuading Sullivan to agree to the old London Prize Ring Rules, Wilson fought Sullivan at Madison Square Garden on the night of July 17, 1882, in a four-round exhibition hypocritically allowed by the mayor, even though prizefighting was still "illegal." According to *The Ring Record Book*, "Tug Collins (Joe Wilson) stayed by hugging and falling to the floor," thus providing Fox with some small satisfaction and Wilson with $1,000 in prize money.

Fox was now aligned with Sullivan's former manager, Billy Madden, who had had a falling out with Sully. Knowing of his pride in everything American, Madden sought to humiliate John L. by bringing over an Englishman to beat him. Madden advertised in the *London Sporting Life* for warm bodies to fight in a heavyweight elimination contest. In Charley Mitchell, a sturdy 158-pounder, Madden found himself a live one. He had beaten the same Tug Wilson that Sullivan had had problems with. Proclaiming Mitchell champion of England, Madden matched him with Sullivan.

The international fight brought a crowd of more than ten thousand to Madison Square Garden. They weren't disappointed. Fighting with gloves under the Queensberry Rules, the lighter Mitchell took the fight to Sullivan and in the very first round, to everyone's surprise, delivered a short right that knocked Sullivan down for the first time in his career. In the third round—after Sullivan had knocked the Englishman through the ropes in the second and out of the ring in the third—the police jumped into the ring. The master of ceremonies—there being no referee—gave Sullivan the decision, although it was a "no decision" bout. Fox had won part of his pound of flesh.

While Sullivan, the invincible, was making short order of any and all that was put in front of him—be they fighters, women, or drinks—Fox continued his search for the elusive golden fleece, a fighter he could fasten his belt and the title "champion" to by besting the Great John L. He imported Herbert A. Slade, a giant Maori, supposedly the best fighter in the Antilles. He lasted three rounds. Next he brought over Al Greenfield, one of England's finest. He went in two.

But Fox was far from through. There now hove onto the horizon a native of Long Island christened John J. Killion, who fought under the name Jake Kilrain. During the early 1880s, Kilrain fought, and beat, some of the best of the heavies, including Jack Burke, Jack Ashton, Frank Herald, and Joe Godfrey among others, and fought a four-round draw with Charley Mitchell. Fox challenged Sullivan to battle and when the champion failed to respond, Fox designated his man, Kilrain, as the recipient of the *Police Gazette* belt, a bauble adorned with diamonds, rubies, and, of course, a picture of Richard Kyle Fox.

Sullivan's legion of fans, angered by Fox's gesture, immediately initiated a drive to raise money to buy their champion a bigger and better belt, in recognition of his claim to the championship being bigger and better. At least, in their eyes. Finally, after raising more than $10,000 they presented their hero with a goldplated belt studded with 350 diamonds, inscribed with the legend "Presented to the champion of champions by the people of the United States." The name John L. Sullivan, properly enough, was outlined in diamonds, with the biggest diamond of all donated by the smallest idolator, Tom Thumb, P. T. Barnum's mighty midget.

Taking the belt, Sullivan wrapped it around his somewhat expanding midriff and bellowed, "Fox's is like a dog collar compared to mine."

But even as he took possession of the magnificent belt presented to him by his followers, the legend of Sully was beginning to become more than a little sullied. First, to support his prodigious appetite for high living, he took to selling off the diamonds, one by one, replacing them with paste. Then, in the same year as the belt presentation, 1887, he met one Patsy Cardiff, the "Peoria Giant." Cardiff was almost an exact replica of another early-day brawler, Tom Sharkey, and a worthy opponent for Sullivan. But worthy or no, Sullivan trained more in the bars of Boston than in the gyms he was less comfortable with. From the very commencement of hostilities Cardiff held his own. Sullivan, unleashing one of his patented left-hand smashes, hit Cardiff atop the head, breaking the champion's arm at the wrist and rendering him hors de combat. Or so the story went when friends of Sullivan's called a halt to the bout after the sixth round. Others, less charitably, ascribed Sullivan's abrupt withdrawal to his lack of condition coupled with the unexpected strength of his opponent.

Meanwhile, Fox had a legitimate claimant to the title. Challenging any living fighter for $5,000 against his $10,000 and finding that Sullivan showed no inclination for such a match, Fox sent Kilrain off to England under the management of Charley Mitchell. There he made a match for Kilrain with the champion of England, Jem Smith. At stake in the first great international battle since Sayers–Heenan was Fox's diamond championship belt. And the reputation of his warrior.

The bout, held on December 19, 1887, at the Isle des Souveraines, River Seine, France, produced few surprises and no winner. Kilrain showed his superiority throughout, but his ignorance of London Prize Fight Rules worked to his disadvantage as his opponent, time and again, took quick falls, ending some rounds in as little as seven to fifteen seconds. Finally after 106 rounds, with both men having sustained much damage—their faces resembling Quasimoto beaten out of all semblance of recognition—the bout was called a "draw" owing to darkness.

Now Fox's campaign against Sullivan picked up momentum. And viciousness. Sullivan, too, picked up, heading for Europe to exploit his popularity, leaving Fox's vituperativeness behind. But first John L. leveled one departing blast: "I've been abused in the papers. I've been lied about and condemned by men who, for commercial reasons, wanted to see some true American, a son of the stars and stripes, whipped by a foreigner. So now I'm intending to get even by unfurling Uncle Sam's victorious flag in the land from which my enemies brought men they hoped would conquer me."

Sullivan's first stop was England. There he met with the warmest welcome ever given an American. Crowds followed him everywhere. And the king of boxing was invited to give an exhibition for the future King of England, the prince of Wales, whom he addressed as "His Princelets." When one of the prince's friends objected to the designation, Sullivan explained he was only doing so because "I heard someone once call the Duke of Argyle 'His Dukelets,' and I thought it would be alright to call the prince 'His Princelets.'" He was admonished by one of his friends not to do it again, "because they're liable to give you a life sentence."

It would be his only social faux pas while in Europe. But not his only problem.

Sullivan's biggest problem was more psychological than physical. He constantly brooded about his antagonist, Richard K. Fox, who had taken a fiendish delight in pelting him with platitudes and bothering him with blatherings. Sullivan, his psyche tortured with tantrums, tried to drown his anguish in drink, if that were possible. He also brooded about the shame of his knockdown at the hands of Mitchell, a mere middleweight.

Finally, a chance came to even the score. He was to get another shot at Mitchell, the man who had humiliated him. And, through Mitchell, at Fox.

Because prizefighting was no longer legal in England, the cradle of boxing, secret arrangements were made to hold the bout in France, a scant three months after the Kilrain–Smith fight on French soil. Scouting around for a site upon which to pitch the ring, the two fighters' parties boarded a train from Paris, and twenty-five miles later hopped off the train in the suburb known as Chantilly. There, on the estate of Baron von Rothschild, on a clean sweep of heather situated between two clumps of trees, they pitched the twenty-four-foot ring on an incline. This latter small detail was the idea of none other than Jake Kilrain, who was seconding Mitchell. He planned to place Mitchell in the corner at the top of the crest of the land if he won the toss, hoping to compensate for Sullivan's advantage in height and reach.

But the loss of the coin toss—and a steady March rain that turned the turf into a quagmire—negated Kilrain's best-laid plans. It didn't matter, however, as Mitchell treated the match less like a fight and more like a footrace, beginning almost imme-diately after "Time" was called to run Sullivan a merry chase. As their spiked shoes ploughed up the rain-soaked ground, the turf soon began to take on the appearance of a pig's wallow. But neither this nor the torrents of rain slowed up Mitchell, who was out to make the bout a cakewalk, sans music. Every now and then Sullivan would stop in his tracks and snarl, "You bloody stiff, why don't you stand up and fight like a man?" But Mitchell would have none of that. After two early knockdowns by Sullivan and "first blood" by Mitchell, the bout became a farce, the only action being that of Sullivan shouting at Mitchell, "Come on and get at me and I'll knock your English block off." But Mitchell was equal to the task, at least of chiding, if not of fighting, and fired back, "Confound it, John, if you don't want to fight we can make it a draw."

Three hours and ten minutes later, with thirty-five seconds thrown in for good measure, the bout was called a draw by mutual agreement. Sullivan was later to say of the 39-round draw, "I might have licked him if I had had a shotgun."

Even with the draw, Sullivan returned home in April of 1888 to a hero's welcome. Immediately, he sought refuge in the only other world he knew, the bottle. After several bouts with a more formidable opponent than he had ever met in the ring, Sullivan collapsed, stricken with a combination of cirrhosis of the liver and typhoid fever. Certainly, the time was right for Fox to once again challenge this physical wreck of a man, the only man who stood between his man, Kilrain, and universal recognition as "heavyweight champion."

With Fox's pink tabloid banging out a constant harangue against the sick champion, who was, according to *The Police Gazette*, "hovering between death's doorstep and taking the back door out of meeting the real champion," Sullivan finally rose to the bait and accepted Fox's challenge to fight Kilrain for the championship and a side bet of $10,000.

But accepting the challenge was only the proverbial ticket to the ball. Now came the most important element of all, getting in shape. It would take a miracle to turn this physical wreck into the fighting machine he had once been, the man once considered invincible before he succumbed to the wages of sin and gin.

Enter William Muldoon, leading physical culturalist of the time, known as "the Noblest Roman of Them All." An awesome physical presence himself, Muldoon immediately tracked down Sullivan in one of his favorite watering holes where he was in the process of drowning his misery in another stein of straight alcohol. Confronting the bloated 237-pound shell of a champion, Muldoon dashed the stein to the floor and physically dragged Sullivan to his health farm at Belfast, New York. There Muldoon performed miracles to rival those of Lourdes, transforming the tottering hulk he found at the bar into a toddling 197-pound bear of a man. All in just six months—in time for Fox and his handpicked gladiator, Jake Kilrain.

With Sullivan ready again to "lick any sonofabitch in the house," especially the one named Kilrain, his devoted followers flocked to New Orleans to see if their man was the Great John L. of old, or whether, as Richard K. Fox continually hinted in unsubtle sallies, an overblown and used-up old man, incapable of defending himself or beating the *Police Gazette*'s "world" champion, Jake Kilrain.

With live wires and deadbeats alike all cramming aboard a train destined for place or places unknown, the special fight trains pulled out of the Queen and Crescent Yards at midnight on July 8, 1889. Riding on the cowcatcher in front of the engine or any place they could cling to under the train, thousands of deadheads forced the train to move at a snail's pace toward its ultimate destination, some one hundred miles away.

Finally, after eight hours and what seemed to be an eternity, the trains lumbered into Richburg, Mississippi, a lumber camp 104 miles north of New Orleans, the final destination and the site of the fight. There, right at the siding, was a twenty-four-foot ring set up in full view on the estate owned by Colonel Charles W. Rich.

Except for a small protuberance in his lower belly, Sullivan hardly looked like the dissipated has-been Fox had painted him to be. His followers installed him as the favorite, though there were those with lingering doubts, like the writer for the *New York World* who mused in print, "According to all such drunkards as he, his legs ought to fail him after twenty minutes of fighting."

At exactly ten minutes after ten o'clock, referee John Fitzpatrick called out "Time!" and the two men advanced to the mark. Rushing out, Kilrain grabbed John L. in a toehold and after much pushing and pulling, hurled him to the ground, falling heavily atop him. The first round had taken all of five seconds. But instead of a look of exultation, there was a look of despair on Jake's face when he returned to his corner. His effort had tired him.

By the fourth round, more frustrated than tired, Sullivan shouted at Kilrain: "Why don't you fight, you sonofabitch? You're the champion, huh? Champion of what?" But Kilrain only laughed and continued, in the best manner of Charley Mitchell, to move away from Sully. It was hauntingly familiar, so much so in fact, that during one clinch Sullivan turned to Mitchell, in Kilrain's corner, and jeered, "Oh, Charley Mitchell, you rat. How I wish I had you in this ring instead of this fellow."

In the seventh a Kilrain roundhouse right landed on Sullivan's ear and as first claret was seen, referee Fitzgerald hollered out "First blood!" and an exchange of bills took place. But it seemed, as round followed round, that Kilrain's strategy was not so much tiring Sullivan as himself. Sullivan even eschewed the time-honored custom of sitting on his second's knee, bellowing, "Why should I? I only have to stand back up again." And when Muldoon asked after the twelfth round how much longer Sullivan could "stay," the indominable Sullivan answered, "Till tomorrow morning, if necessary."

Soon the battle and the heat began to wear down both battlers. A blazing sun and a temperature of 104 degrees made it one of the hottest July days in memory. And were one to ask, "How hot was it?" one only would have had to look at Chief Hughes, who was Sullivan's bottlewasher. "Maje," as he was called, stood bareheaded in Sully's corner. As the fight progressed his bald head began to blister and his scalp started to balloon up. By the twenty-seventh round, the balloon burst, and there on Maje's head could be seen, in Sully's words, "the nicest crop of hair you ever saw."

Sullivan decked Kilrain in the twenty-seventh round. But then the fight reverted to form—Kilrain's form—and the slow pace resumed. After the forty-third round, Muldoon slipped Sullivan some tea laced with whiskey; Sullivan almost immediately took ill and vomited, ridding himself of the tea, the whiskey, and, apparently, all other vestigal remainders of his fatigue. When Kilrain asked him, "You wanta go quit?" Sullivan bellowed "No!" and punctuated his answer with a straight right. It knocked Kilrain to the turf.

Now it was only a matter of time, and, as the fight continued, the result was becoming more and more apparent. As the exhausted Kilrain was dragged to his corner at the end of the seventy-fifth round, his head rolling loosely as if it were broken, a physician, after examining the broken and beaten warrior, informed Donovan, "If you keep sending that man of yours in he will surely drop dead of exhaustion."

After two hours and sixteen minutes, give or take a few, Donovan threw in the sponge as a symbol of his defeat. John L. Sullivan had again emerged triumphant.

The last great bareknuckle fight was now history. And an age that had started 170 years before on a wooden stage at James

Figg's Amphitheatre ended on a clearing in Richburg, Mississippi. The first great act in the continuing drama known as boxing was over. And with it, although it was not known at the time, was the age of one of the greatest men ever to touch the sport: The age of John L. Sullivan.

JACK JOHNSON: BLACK CHAMPION AND WHITE HOPES

In the world of the early 1900s, still awash with Victorian gentility and doily-type embroidery on everything from manners and modes to conversation and conventional heroes, the heavyweight champion's name stood out in stark relief, a man of swaggering virility who epitomized the turbulent, yet proud, surety of the populace of a nation destined for greatness.

However, with Jim Jeffries's retirement, no longer was there one man who could lay claim to the title of "the strongest man in the world"; no longer one man at the top of boxing's mountain. In more ways than one, boxing had plunged into a period of darkness.

Jeffries had tried, in his own naive way, to perpetuate the heavyweight title, by personally handing over his title to the winner of a fight between Marvin Hart and light heavyweight champion Jack Root. But heavyweight championships are not looked upon as a matter of birthright, to be passed on, like the British crown. They are to be won in the ring, and Hart's ascension to the throne was received with one giant yawn.

Meanwhile, in the words of one of those Sweet Caporal cigarette buttons then being worn by some of the so-called gay blades,
the year 1906 "just had to get better, 'cause it can't get worse."
An economic downturn lay on the land. The United States was
suffering through its second depression in ten years—this time
complete with millions out of work and the first bread lines in
American history.

It was just such a rare combination of occurrences—Jeffries's
abdication coupled with the economic muting of vox populi—
that gave form and flight to those divisions, which had been relegated to the back of boxing's bus, and now came forward to take
their places in the limelight, led by the lightweight division.

The one man who would make the lightweights a major
attraction, and make a lasting contribution to boxing, was a sourdough named George L. ("Tex") Rickard. Rickard had gone to
Alaska in search of gold, glory, and God-blessed fun, and found a
little of all three as he alternated between bust and boom, opening and closing saloons with the same frequency as gold veins
were found. Rickard found that the Klondike was a man's world,
not because of chauvinism, necessarily, but because there literally were no women to be found. Men were reduced to making their own entertainment, whether it was bellying up to the
bar night after night, dancing with the house girls at saloons, or
merely seeking out stage shows and other amusements. One such
amusement was boxing, a discovery made by Rickard, as valuable
as any by a sourdough.

In 1902, after seven long years in Alaska, Rickard decided it
was time to cash in his chips and move along. He took $65,000
with him and looked for something else. That something else
included a side trip to San Francisco in an attempt to catch a
glimpse of the man Rickard called "my idol, 'Gentleman Jim'

Corbett." In 1904 Rickard left for Nevada, having heard of a new gold strike in a town aptly named Goldfield.

Everyone seemed drawn to Goldfield. To a nation suffering through a major depression, the news that one mine produced more than $5 million of gold-bearing ore in three months brought thousands to the tent city pretentiously called "the greatest mining camp ever known."

Seeking more lucrative ways to attract the world's attention to their dusty little El Dorado, the town fathers, including Rickard, met to consider such ideas as a man-made lake filled with beer; a hot-air balloon with a basket filled with ten-dollar gold pieces that would be thrown down onto Goldfield's streets; a racetrack stocked with camels imported from the Sahara, and so on. Rickard suggested a prizefight.

The men formed the Goldfield Athletic Club the same day and raised $50,000 to back a fight. Their work done, Rickard was appointed to the joint positions of treasurer and promoter. He would be responsible for finding the fighters, negotiating the contracts, and erecting the arena.

Rickard had his work cut out for him. First he wired the managers of Jimmy Britt, claimant to the lightweight crown, and "Terrible" Terry McGovern, former bantamweight and featherweight champion, offering, "fifteen thousand dollars for a fight to the finish." In those days of fighting for a percentage of the gate, such an offer was unheard of. So too was Tex Rickard. No one responded. Thinking he had to increase the ante, Rickard wired Battling Nelson, who had just beaten Britt for something called "the white lightweight championship of the world," an offer of $20,000 for a "finish fight" against the recognized titleholder, Joe Gans. Still, no answer. But Rickard wouldn't take "no answer" for an answer; he just went straight to the champion, Gans. Gans, having just knocked out Mike "Twin" Sullivan, was badly in need of money, having been left high and dry by his less-than-savory manager. Now acting as his own manager, Gans immediately wired back his acceptance, agreeing to any terms Nelson demanded.

With Gans in the fold, Rickard left for Reno to begin construction of an arena. While there he heard that although his offer of $20,000 to Nelson was the largest guarantee ever offered, the number-one fight promoter in the country, Sunny Jim Coffroth, was heading east to meet Gans and offer him more. Realizing he was fast becoming an almost-promoter, Rickard increased his offer to the unheard-of-sum of $30,000. When he returned to Goldfield he found a telegram from Nelson's manager, accepting the bid for the fight, the only stipulation being that Nelson get two-thirds of the total guarantee.

Oscar Battling Matthew Nelson was more simply known as "Bat" or "the Durable Dane." His head was said to be invulnerable to punishment due to the triple-thick Neanderthal construction of his cranium. Typically he took about three punches to every one he landed. His favorite punch—to the kidneys—probably helped earn him a reputation for being less than a gentleman. He liked to use every trick in the book and some that weren't, including gouging, butting, and dirty in-fighting.

Joe Gans, on the other glove, was one of the classic boxers of all time, called—even today—one of the greatest boxer pound-for-pound and punch-for-punch of all time. In his 144 fights before Goldfield, Gans had scored forty-nine knockouts—including a one-round knockout of Frank Erne to win the lightweight title four years earlier—against just five losses. And three of those losses were tainted to satisfy the betting whims of his manager, Al Herford. Now impoverished and unable to get fights, the "Old Master" agreed to each new division of the guarantee Nelson's manager demanded, finally settling for $10,000 to Nelson's $23,000, an amount Rickard stacked up in newly minted, double-eagle gold pieces in the local bank's window.

The day of the fight almost eight thousand fans—among them three hundred women, the first time they had shown up in any number at an exhibition of the "gentlemanly" art of self-defense—made their way into the newly-constructed arena.

Gans, seriously weakened by having to make the weight just minutes before fight time (something insisted upon by Nelson's manager), was the first to enter the eighteen-foot ring (another concession to Nelson). He was still clutching a poignant telegram he had received from his mother in Baltimore: "Joe, the eyes of the world are on you. Everybody says you ought to win. Peter Jackson will tell me the news. You bring back the bacon." Battling Nelson, confident as always, entered next.

For the first ten rounds, his lithe black body glistening under the boiling Nevada sun, Gans exhibited a masterful display of boxing skills. In the eleventh Bat gained control with his stylized roughhousing.

By the forty-first round, it was obvious even to Nelson that his "dirty" techniques were not enough. In the forty-second, while Gans attempted to smother Nelson's cuffing and gouging, the challenger began raining blows somewhere south of Gans's beltline. As referee George Siler was in the process of issuing a stern warning to Nelson, Nelson drove his right hand into Gans's groin. Siler pushed Nelson to his corner, returned to the stricken champion, and raised his arm. In the longest championship fight in Marquess of Queensberry history, Gans was the winner and still lightweight champion. On a foul.

And, just as importantly, he was able to wire his mother after the fight: "Mammy, your boy is bringing home the bacon with lots of gravy on it."

Boxing was to have several other bouts that begot gravy as well, but, unfortunately, none in the heavyweight division. While the lightweight division sported such great names as Nelson, Gans, and Al Wolgast, the Michigan Wildcat, the featherweight division possessed the likes of Abe Attell and Young Corbett; the welterweight division numbered among its top names Honey Mellody and the Dixie Kid; and the middleweight division had such luminaries as Stanley Ketchel and Billy Papke. The heavyweight crown, such as it was, was worn by five-foot, seven-inch, 179-pound Noah Brusso, who fought under the nom de guerre of Tommy Burns. It was his misfortune to be a mere bridge to history, a waystation between greats.

The heavyweight "crown," personally presented to Marvin Hart on the occasion of his upset win over Jack Root by none other than the retiring champion, Jim Jeffries, passed on to Tommy Burns in Hart's first defense. Most fight fans still did not accept Burns, feeling that Jeff was still the real champion and that Hart, and now Burns, were merely custodians of the crown until his return.

Nothing Burns did could change their opinion of him. He fought and beat the best American heavyweights around, such as they were, in Fireman Jim Flynn and Philadelphia Jack O'Brien, the light heavyweight champion. Still, his dubious claim to the championship was greeted by an overwhelming apathy that rivaled the sound of one hand applauding.

And so, in keeping with the Biblical passage that holds that a prophet is not without honor except in his own country, Burns took the road several entertainers had at the turn of the century—he traveled abroad. Thus, while ranked as a minor talent at home, Burns was praised and applauded abroad. He met, and in quick succession knocked out, Gunner Moir, Jack Palmer, and Jem Roche in Great Britain, then traveled to France where he faced the likes of Jewey Smith and Bill Squires, adding them to his growing list of KO victims, and then, finally, traveled to Australia, where he knocked out Bill Squires for the third time, and Bill Lang, making it eight straight knockouts in defense of his slightly tainted crown.

But it wasn't so much that Tommy Burns had won the heavyweight championship and wanted to see the world that had transported him to faraway places; it was the presence of a dark shadow in the United States—the shadow of one John Arthur Johnson, better known as Jack Johnson, "the Galveston Giant."

To assess Jack Johnson's place in boxing history is as difficult as attempting to categorize Shakespeare's Othello merely as a Moor. And as misleading. The rise and fall of Jack Johnson was as shaped by his blackness as by America's reaction to his blackness; and, in many ways, it was as much a preordained tragedy as that of Othello.

Ever since John L. Sullivan had invoked the color line— challenging "any and all bluffers" to meet him, then adding the caveat, "I will not fight a Negro. I never have and I never will"— blacks had been denied the right to fight for the heavyweight title. They were boxing's, if not society's, invisible people. Assuredly, there had been black champions—Barbados Joe Walcott, Joe Gans, and Dixie Kid—but no heavyweight champion, the supposed symbol of the strongest man in the world and ruler of all he surveyed. Fighting a black man was perfectly acceptable for those trying to make a name for themselves, as when Corbett met Peter Jackson. But the heavyweight champion was not to fight a black man; it was the unwritten law. There was everything to lose and nothing to gain.

Jack Johnson would change all that, just as he would many of America's perceptions of the black man, savaging their sons and ravaging their daughters as he flaunted every convention set out to intercept just such an interloper.

Denied his chance to find his roots in big-time boxing, Johnson blossomed in bootleg fights, Battle Royals—a barbaric pastime indulged in by many communities which saw between six and eight fighters, all blindfolded and almost all black, fight until the last man left standing was adjudged the winner—on the Chitlin' Circuit against other blacks, where his life was an endless chain of rundown rooming houses, broken-down buses, and foul-smelling beaneries.

Relegated into their own isolated world, some black heavyweights had gained a measure of celebrity: Peter Jackson, Sam Langford, Sam McVey, and Joe Jeanette, to name a few. But few got further than that. Now Johnson sought to defy one of boxing's ineluctable verities—that no black man could become heavyweight champion of the world.

Beginning his career in 1897, the year Fitzsimmons dethroned Corbett, Johnson had a measure of success at first, fighting in and around Galveston, Texas. But the real beginning came when two of boxing's all-time greats—Barbados Joe Walcott and Joe Choynski—took a personal interest in the Galveston Giant or, as he had taken to calling himself, "'Lil Arthur."

Johnson had trained with Walcott, the great master, when Walcott was in training for a title fight; Choynski, on the other hand, had an adversarial relationship with Johnson—at least for three rounds, that is. For that was the amount of time the old war horse needed to catch the youngster on the temple and knock him to the ground. Almost before Johnson's face had settled in the dirt, Texas Rangers had overrun the ring, arresting all within

sight for participating in an illegal prizefight. The two most notable of the arrestees were Choynski and Johnson, both of whom
were sentenced to jail for breaking the law. It was there, in the
exercise yard of the local hoosegow, that Choynski imparted
some valuable tips to his willing student.

Johnson was to meld together everything Walcott and
Choynski had "larned" him, translating their styles into his own,
one characterized by the ability to counterpunch brilliantly with
a defense that was well-nigh impregnable. Coupled with his
enormous strength, which some critics said gave him the ability
to name the punch that would take a man out, and catlike moves,
Johnson was almost unbeatable and well on his way to becoming
one of boxing's all-time greats.

After being released, Johnson stayed in Galveston only long
enough to pack, taking the next train to Chicago, where he hoped
to get some fights with top-ranking boxers. Instead, too black
and too dangerous for Chicago promoters, Johnson nearly froze
to death in squatter's shacks before giving up and heading west
in quest of fights. There his luck improved—he started getting
decent matches and winning them, beating the likes of George
Gardner, who had defeated Joe Walcott; Sam McVey; and Denver Ed Martin, for what was called "The Negro Heavyweight
Championship."

But it was the world's heavyweight championship he coveted,
not just the Negro heavyweight championship. And the only way
to win it was to meet and beat the champion, James J. Jeffries. So
Johnson, as he was always to do, did the unthinkable: he walked
into Jeff's San Francisco saloon to challenge him.

Entering Jeffries's saloon, he found the great man at the bar
and, as the story goes, walked up to him and demanded a shot at
the title then held by Jeff. Jeff, who told the story in later years,

remembered that all he knew of the big man facing him was that he had lost to Choynski. He stared at the audacious apparition in front of him for a moment and then said, "I won't meet you in the ring 'cause you've got no name and we wouldn't draw flies. But," the champion remembered saying, "I'll tell you what I'll do . . . I'll go downstairs to the cellar with you and lock the door from the inside. And the one who comes out with the key will be the champ." Johnson couldn't believe the champ was serious. "Oh I am, I am," said Jeff. "And I'll do it right now!" With that, Johnson turned and walked away, his bluff called, and his first challenge for a shot at the championship denied. But he would try and try again.

Jack now wanted three things: revenge for Jeff's slight, a reputation, and, most importantly, the world's heavyweight title. The first he got in his very next fight, against Jeffries's younger brother, Jack, whom he knocked out in five; the reputation continued to come as he won bout after bout on his way through the heavyweight division; but the heavyweight title shot he coveted so dearly was no closer.

His chances seemed to recede, if anything, when he met Marvin Hart in early 1905, the same year Hart would be dubbed by Jeffries as his successor. The 26-year-old, six-foot-one, one-quarter-inches, 210-pound, finely-tuned Johnson manhandled his lighter and smaller opponent and yet lost a decision to a bloodied and battered Hart when the referee mysteriously awarded the fight to a man who resembled a loser in every way but in the final decision. Bitter, but unable to do anything to reverse a miscarriage of justice, Johnson vowed never to let a close bout go to decision again.

By the time Hart relinquished his crown to Burns, Johnson had beaten everyone who would get in the ring with him, including the great Boston Tar Baby, Sam Langford. Yet his goal continued to elude him. Burns did everything within his power to forestall meeting this man who was menacing the heavyweight division like Tamerlane the Tartar and his yellow hordes had menaced the populace in the fourteenth century, including taking his "championship" on a worldwide tour, far from the threat of Johnson. Johnson took off in pursuit of the crown he knew he was always meant to wear.

While Burns was fattening his record on a long list of mediocrities, Johnson was beating the likes of Bob Fitzsimmons, Sam Langford, Joe Jeanette, and Jim Flynn, all victims of what the papers called "the playful Ethiopian." One English paper, the prestigious *Mirror of Life and Boxing World*, said that the man who had issued public challenges to no less than three reigning heavyweight champions would, if he ever met Burns, be "his master."

Finally, halfway around the world, in the unlikely spot of Sydney, Australia, Johnson got his long-awaited shot. But it was not so much the challenger who forced the issue, as Burns, who succumbed to the dual blandishments of public opinion and the monetary rewards offered by Australian promoter H. D. ("Huge Deal") McIntosh. McIntosh made the largest guarantee ever made to a heavyweight champion—the unheard-of amount of $35,000—leaving only the crumbs, some $6,000 worth, for Johnson.

Burns, firing off virulent salvos of racial slurs, as was the custom of the day, made outrageous demands on McIntosh and Johnson, all of which were accepted: he dictated the choice of ring size, the date of the fight—Boxing Day, the day after Christmas, 1908—and the naming of the referee, the very same H. D. McIntosh, considered by all to be Burns's "friend." Moreover, he insisted that the fight go to a decision, no matter what. If all these demands were meant as bluffs, Johnson called them all. He wanted the fight in the worst way. Some thought that's how he got it, including the gamblers, who installed the champion as the 7–4 favorite, with very little Johnson money to be found anywhere.

On Boxing Day, at approximately one minute of eleven under a hot Australian summer sun, the six-foot-one-and-one-half inches, 195-pound challenger entered the ring first, as was his wont, preceded through the ropes by his manager, Sam Fitzpatrick, and succeeded by overwhelming silence from the crowd of forty thousand. Burns, the five-foot-seven-and-one-half inches, 180-pound champion, defending his title for the twelfth time, climbed into the ring three minutes later to resounding cheers emanating from the forest of white faces in the specially constructed arena at Rushcutter's Bay.

The fight was, in the words of novelist Jack London, covering the match for the *New York Herald,* "No fight." Instead, this boxing match-hyphen-sociological struggle was one of the cruelest scenes ever played out within the confines of a ring, a play that would have made the Marquis de Sade proud.

From the very first punch, a long left by Johnson, to the end of the fight some fourteen rounds later, the Galveston Giant played out his one-and-a-half years of frustration in a manner never before seen, taunting his smaller opponent, who was outweighed and outgunned in every department, except, ironically, in reach; Burns's 74½-inch reach was almost two inches longer than his six-inch taller opponent's. Johnson leered at him, the hot sun reflecting off his bared gold teeth, and jeered at him with remarks that amounted to verbal winks—"Come on leedle Tahmmy, come right here where I want you"—all the while pushing Burns around at will. During the brief interludes when he tied up the advancing champion, he would talk to the press and once even expectorated over the heads of the all-white press corps. Occasionally he would indulge in a semi-obligatory pugilistic interlude, lacing Burns unmercifully with combinations.

The worst fears of white men everywhere were confirmed as Burns tried time and again to penetrate the impenetrable defenses of the big black man and was rebuffed by masterful counterpunches or tied up, helpless as a small white mouse in the hands of a large black cat. Burns never could get to his challenger-cum-tormentor, who spent much of the afternoon ridiculing the champion, his pitiable efforts, and his followers.

For thirteen rounds Johnson was insufferable. And unbeatable. As "time" for the fourteenth round was called, an exhausted Burns had barely gotten off his stool when he was met by Johnson. Burns warily moved away as Johnson stalked his opponent, sure of himself and his ultimate victory. He threw a straight right to the head, dropping Burns heavily. As McIntosh counted, Burns raised himself to his haunches and slowly regained his feet at "eight," arising only to find Johnson, who had been standing over him, on him at once like a panther, battering the soon-to-be-ex-champ at will.

With Burns tottering helplessly, unable to defend himself and leaning against the ropes in an attempt to avert Johnson's heavy blows, the Sydney police took matters into their own hands, rushing into the ring, shutting off the movie cameras and mercifully stopping the fight. It having been previously decided that if the police intervened a decision would be rendered on points, referee McIntosh walked over and held the hand of Johnson aloft, signifying his victory—and his becoming the new heavyweight champion of the world.

The stoppage of the fight unleashed a tide of hatred. It was unthinkable that the white man's burden had become his master; that the so-called inferior race was superior to the white man in this, the most supreme of all contests between two men. Suddenly, the man who represented the strongest, most powerful, and most visible figure in the world was black.

Disbelief refused to suspend itself. With sanctimonious smugness, white men everywhere demanded that other white men, called, for lack of a better name, "White Hopes," rescue back their title, their heritage, to take it away from this defiler of all that was sacred.

Jack London sounded the first call to arms in his closing paragraph from Sydney, demanding that Jim Jeffries "must emerge from his alfalfa farm and remove that smile from Johnson's face." His call was like a pebble thrown into a pond, as the ripples reached every corner of the world and a grizzled collection of ranch hands, gandy dancers, rodeo riders, carpenters, plowboys, and all manner of men joined in the crusade to avenge what they considered to be an historical inaccuracy. All hardy, if not foolhardy, they became part of one of boxing's longest-running spectacles—the finding of a "White Hope," a title given to any fighter of more than 175 pounds and the right complexion, all the better to throw the rascal out.

And Johnson just might have been that rascal. At least, according to most observers. A subtle spirit defiant, he lived the life of fast women, fast cars, and sloe gin, flaunting every excess to excess and living life to the fullest. But his high style of living, his marriages to three white women, and his opening of a nightclub in Chicago—the freewheeling Café de Champion, which served all comers and none of society's mores—brought, like decaying fish, the redolent stench of scandal to the nostrils of the moralists. He was a national hero unworthy of his position and one who had to be disposed of.

But who could beat this man whose fighting style was unbeatable, whose defense made him unhittable, and whose catlike movements and counterpunching abilities made any opponent's chances against him unthinkable? Especially when the "White Hopes" merely proved out Gresham's law of bad heavyweights, the bad ones forcing out the good ones.

And so it was, with the heavyweight division devoid of hope or hopes, that the first man to challenge Johnson was the middleweight champion of the world, Stanley Ketchel, in an attempt to duplicate Bob Fitzsimmons's feat of leapfrogging from the middleweight to the heavyweight title just twelve years before.

Stanley Ketchel was the stuff dreams—and legends—are made of. Born Stanislaus Kiecal on a Michigan farm of a Russian father and a 14-year-old Polish mother, he ran away at 14, rode the rails, and lived the life of a hobo, picking up fighting as a saloon bouncer in Butte, Montana, where he fought any and all for pocket money. Or fun. He claimed 250 fights before the first official one showed up in *The Ring Record Book*. But in all of his matches, recorded or no, his blond hair and handsome face radiated a ferocity that only Jack Dempsey was later to match. He made one believe he wanted to kill; hence his nickname, "the Michigan Assassin," came closer to reflecting his style of fighting than most ring nicknames.

Called by Philadelphia Jack O'Brien, a man he twice rendered hors de combat, "an example of tumultuous ferocity," Ketchel had raced through the middleweight division, denuding it of competition, knocking out forty-seven of his sixty opponents. Only once had he been knocked out, by Billy Papke in defense of his title when, as Ketchel reached out to shake Papke's hand at the commencement of hostilities Papke responded by catching Ketchel in the windpipe with a murderous right. Still, even though Ketchel went down four times in the first and was literally beaten to a bloody pulp, it took Papke fourteen rounds to finish this man who possessed what some called "the soul of a bouncer." With the words "Shake hands and come out fighting" now part of boxing's lexicon as a result of his loss, Ketchel came back just eighty days later to knock Papke out, taking one less round to avenge his loss—a loss that would have forced most fighters into retirement. But not Stanley Ketchel.

In Ketchel the fanatics had finally found their hope, the man they believed could reclaim their heavyweight championship. But an air of improbability surrounded the fight. On the one hand there was the middleweight champion of the world, only five feet, nine inches tall, and weighing all of 154 pounds. On the other, was the man known as "the Galveston Giant," a strapping six-foot-plus, 200-pound tree of a man who had made short work of all served up to him of equal size, let alone smaller men, like Tommy Burns. In order to minimize the size and weight differences, all publicity shots between the two had Ketchel posing in overstuffed greatcoats, and wearing five-inch heels to lend some stature to the dimensions.

But if there was an aura of improbability to their dimensions, it was heightened by the rumors of the improbability of the fight itself, one which was suggested to be less than on the level. It was widely believed by many that Johnson had agreed to carry his smaller foe for the sake of the movie cameras. And Johnson himself, who was not above spinning a good tale, later wrote that he had to do something to make the fight interesting, like "pretending" to go down and then getting back up to knock out Ketchel.

Regardless of the recurring rumors, a watchful nation held its collective breath as Johnson defended his title for the first time on October 16, 1909 against Ketchel and more than ten thousand hopeful fans crowded into the Colma, California arena to see Johnson get his due. Ketchel, sure of himself and his destiny, sat in the dressing room smoking a cigarette and regaling all in attendance with a funny story, until one of his handlers told him it was "time to go to work." The Panlike Ketchel blissfully ignored the summons and finished his story and his cigarette unhurriedly. Then, and only then, he stood up. "Come on," he told his entourage, "let's go out there and finish that skunk!"

But whether Ketchel did not know that he was merely a bit player in a scenario especially made for the movies or had merely forgotten his part is not known. What is known is that he didn't settle for his role as second banana and started to ad lib his part. And only when he did so did Johnson react, three times to be exact. For the remainder of the fight, it was quite evident, as the reporter for *The New York Times* noted, that "Johnson appeared to be holding himself back all the time."

Finally, after eleven rounds of what could charitably be called sparring, the two combatants answered the bell for the fateful twelfth round. The minute it rang Ketchel jumped from his stool and went out to meet his rival. Johnson, with his hands held high to catch Ketchel's forays, met his assault with a straight left, momentarily arresting Ketchel's movement, then grabbed and wrestled Ketchel to Johnson's corner. As the two men broke away, Johnson poised and, with a pantherlike leap, sprang to meet Ketchel. Ketchel, reacting to Johnson's sudden move as well as to a verbal prod which came from his corner in a singsong voice pleading for him to "Come on now, Stanley!" threw a sweeping right hand up over the top. Johnson ducked and Ketchel's right serpentined around the back of Johnson's neck, looking as if it hit him on the ear. Johnson lost his balance and toppled toward the canvas, holding himself up with his outstretched left glove and never really hitting the floor. Johnson leaped up, a malevolent grin on his face as Ketchel raced in to put the finishing touches on his partially completed work. As Ketchel leaped forward, Johnson shot out his right fist, catching the oncoming Ketchel on the jaw. Simultaneously, he threw a left to the pit of the challenger's stomach. Ketchel fell heavily, as if he had been poleaxed, his arms and legs outstretched in a perfect five-point star.

The momentum of his efforts carried Johnson through and over the stricken Ketchel, forcing him to stumble on the fallen form. He hurriedly jumped up and, picking two of Ketchel's teeth out of his right glove, stood legs crossed, with one hand on the ropes, the other on his hip, content with an afternoon's work. An excellent movie "take." When asked later how he felt being knocked down, Johnson gave further substantiation to the prefight rumors by answering, "Far better than Ketchel did thirty seconds later. He crossed me and I made him pay for it."

As the now-silent crowd filed out of the Colma arena, its hopes as crushed as Ketchel's teeth, the call went out for Jim Jeffries. He was the one man who could beat Johnson, and, the faithful held, the "real" champion because he had not been beaten in the ring, but had turned over his title to Marvin Hart for safe-keeping. Hart, of course, had lost it to Burns, who had, in turn, lost it to Johnson. But they were not the real champions: Jeffries was. And he would beat this pretender to his throne—this black man wearing the white man's crown.

Only the invincible Jeff, the chosen representative of the white race, could answer for the real and imagined slights the Caucasian psyche had suffered at the hands of this black who was living life to the fullest and flaunting his color in the white man's face. Not the white hopes and the white hopeless. It had to be Jeff.

Now he heeded the clarion call to arms. He would return from his alfalfa farm and recapture "his" crown, even if he had to shed close to a hundred pounds to do so. He became the Great

White Hope, the Great White Prayer. And he would do his duty as his public saw fit.

This was more than a classic match-up. This was a morality play. Black versus white. Invader versus avenger. And no one grasped the marketing potential of the match better than Tex Rickard. He eagerly sought to become its architect, but he was not alone. Others saw its inherent drama and profit. Representatives of both fighters met and agreed to a bout to be held in July 1910. They stipulated that all bids for the bout must be submitted to them on December 1, 1909, in New York. The "promoters" came out of the proverbial woodwork.

It was Rickard who saw that whoever had the champion had the fight as well. He made a pilgrimage to Pittsburgh, like one of the faithful visiting Lourdes hoping to be blessed, to catch up with Johnson. There he found the champion, whose big spending had left him broke, taking his turn on the vaudeville circuit—skipping rope, punching the bag, amusing audiences with stories and playing a bull fiddle. When Rickard approached him backstage, Johnson greeted him with, "This is the situation, Mr. Tex. No matter what the papers say about the big money for the fight, nothin' is set. Now, what would be helpful to me is about twenty-five hundred to settle up some bills and damn all." Seeing his opening, Rickard reached into his greatcoat and peeled two thousand-dollar bills and a five hundred from his roll and handed them to the wide-eyed champion whose face broke into the golden smile Jack London—and all the world—had come to abhor. There was no signature, no handshake. But from that moment on Rickard had the champion, and the fight—a fight he nailed down by offering a $170,000 purse, seventy-five percent to the winner, which Jeffries later changed to a sixty percent-forty percent split, and $10,000 under the table to each man.

Now he had to find a site. Originally he planned to have the fight in California, which, at the time was the mecca for big-time boxing, especially championship fights, the Johnson–Ketchel fight having been held there only the year before. But reform was on the move in 1910. State after state passed legislation forbidding drinking, prizefighting, and just about anything else that smacked of fun. Even the pedestrian painting *September Morn*—later to become a logo for White Rock beverages—had been banned by Watch and Ward Societies for promiscuously showing a nude young lady standing on a rock. But Jack Johnson gave the reformers a cause greater than most. White against black was unnatural, or so the reasoning went. Intimating that no white woman was safe in her own boudoir—intermingling choice words like "miscegenation" and "mongrelization"—the reformers set upon California's Governor James J. Gillette to ban the fight.

Coupled with the invasion of their borders by the black champion was something equally pernicious—rumors of a fixed fight. The betting crowd was convinced that the "fix was in." It supposedly had been arranged for Jeffries to win, with the black champion to take a "dive." As rumors of fix and the rumbles of the reformers reached his ears with an ever-increasing din, the governor saw political wisdom in throwing the fight out of his state.

But if California didn't want him, Rickard's old home state of Nevada did—especially Reno, which Rickard selected "because more railroads junction here." And Reno it was, where, on a hot, sultry Independence Day, 1910, the first "Fight of the Century" took place.

Everyone who was anyone was there, and some nobodies as well. One journalist noted, "Pugs, gamblers, newspaper reporters, scrubs, whores, and sons of bitches in plenty" roamed the streets.

They were there to witness the day when all would be set right, when Jeff would once again prove to be invincible.

In the name of solidarity, Jim Corbett and John L. Sullivan shook hands and ended their eighteen-year feud to both back Jeff. Bettors, too, backed Jeff, to the tune of 10–7, believing the Easter Bunny–esque tale that he was, as the press would tell its believing public, "in the best shape of his life." But the man who had been coaxed out of retirement and who had shed almost a hundred pounds bore little resemblance to the man who had last put on gloves some six years before; his vaunted left was now only a memory, his once-great strength now a victim of the passage of time. In short, he was a sham. But nobody wanted to believe it. They took as an article of faith that a white man, no matter how old or out of shape, was superior in every way to his obviously inferior counterpart—especially this one, the one with the infamous golden smile.

But Jeffries knew, all too well. The man who had been supremely confident in each of his previous fights could not sleep the night before the bout, pacing his room like a caged tiger. He also knew something nobody else could have even guessed. When the fight moved from California to Nevada, the "arrangement" that Jeffries would win was called off. Johnson had sent him word that he was no longer bound by the secret prefight agreement to "go into the tank." Now it was "best man wins," and Jeff knew before he entered the ring that Johnson was that best man.

But, for the hopeful crowd of 15,760 jammed cheek-by-jowl into the amphitheater of yellow pine—and the 2,000 plus members of the press corps from every corner of the white man's world—the hoped-for never came. As they roared their support of Jeff, and cornerman Jim Corbett exhorted his friend and charge to "Use the one-two, Jeff, the one-two," Johnson showed his mastery by stifling everything Jeffries did, then, pushing him back and keeping his opponent at cautious arm's length, all the while taunting Jeff, the press and his cornermen, singled out Corbett for special abuse. Tied up and frustrated, Jeffries began to take on the look of a boxing version of Dorian Gray, aging right before the eyes of his faithful. The realization that their hero was not the man he had been slowly began to dawn on the crowd. Their disappointment took voice in their pleas, "Jeff, it's up to you."

Finally, in the fifteenth, Johnson ended their hopes forever, flooring Jeff for the first time in his career with a right uppercut and three lefts and then beating him through the ropes with one thunderous left. After being gingerly helped to his feet by his cornermen and shoved back into the path of the advancing panther, Jeffries sank to the canvas under the collective onslaught of five left hooks. He hung on to the ropes and gasped for breath. Amid screams of "Stop it! Stop it!" from the disheartened, Tex Rickard, now acting in his capacity as referee, walked over and held up Johnson's hand. The crusade had failed. The Greek drama had turned into a tragedy.

The defeat of Jeffries sparked riots in many American cities, riots that left almost thirty people dead. In New York, Washington, Omaha, Little Rock, Houston, and all points, north, east, south, and west, whites watched in stunned horror as blacks paraded through the streets proclaiming their superiority. It was a terrible blow to a society dedicated to "keeping those people in their place," a wound to their psyche which was now ripped open and rubbed raw by the ostentatiousness of Johnson and those who celebrated his victory.

Had there been a Nobel Prize for dividing the races, Jack Johnson would have won it, gloves down. After winning the title from Burns, he had told his then-manager, Sam Fitzpat-rick, "I'll make them [the whites] kowtow to me. I'll make them small beer." He outraged both races by making his own rules. He married three white women, one of whom, Etta Duryea, took her own life. Johnson later lamented, "She was murdered by the world, by spiteful tongues, by my enemies, by racial hatred." But this firebrand also fueled the fires of racial hatred himself. Booker T. Washington, one of the black leaders of the time, told an audience, "I'm sure that they [Johnson's actions] do not meet the approval of the colored race." Still, he was the cock of the walk, and it wasn't the "coon walk," or the dirt area bordering the street where blacks were required to walk in many cities; it was the center of the street, the main walk. He was one "uppity nigger" who didn't know his place, "ten miles of bad road," in the black vernacular of the day. And that hurt. Both races.

When, only two years earlier, Theodore Roosevelt had Booker T. Washington at the White House for lunch, "Pitchfork" Ben Tillman, the senator from Mississippi, had said, "Washing-ton is a good man, but his going to the White House means we're going to have to lynch a few more nigras to keep 'em in their place." Now they were going to have to lynch Jack Johnson to keep him in his.

And so, what man couldn't do, the government now attempted to do: get Jack Johnson. Declaring that Independence Day had been dishonored and disgraced by a brutal prizefight and that the moral sense of the nation had been outraged, state-after-state took the pathetic stand of banning the exhibition of moving pic-tures of the fight on the stated belief that their showing would incite further rioting. And, as if to complete their paroxysm of anger, they enacted legislation designed to forbid interracial fights and interracial marriages as well.

But the final blow to be struck against Johnson and his antisocial ways was the enforcement of a law passed in 1910—originally intended to prohibit the transportation of women across state lines for immoral purposes—called the Mann Act, or more familiarly, the White Slavery Act.

Casting about for a likely prospect to testify against Johnson, they found Belle Schreiber, a self-acknowledged prostitute whom Johnson had taken to California for companionship during his training for Jeffries. Based on her testimony, a jury deliberated less than two hours before finding Johnson guilty of transporting the unfair Belle across state lines for the stated purposes of "prostitution, debauchery, committing a crime against nature, and unlawful sexual intercourse," despite her admission that she had gone willingly. The heavyweight champion was sentenced to one year and one day in Joliet prison and a fine of $1,000.

Released to settle his affairs, Johnson jumped bail. Vowing never to return to the United States, he began a less-than-grand tour of Europe. There, a man without a country, a la Edward Everett Hale's famous literary figure, Johnson soon found himself out of money, out of contact, and out of sorts. He took anything in order to afford himself the manner to which he had become accustomed. He played the vaudeville circuit, wrestled a Russian, and fought Frank Moran in a lackluster 20-round fight in defense of his title. But when he was unable to collect his portion of the purse because of litigation, wanderlust set in, and he lit out again, this time for South America. And ultimately, Havana.

The "White Hope" movement, born out of the belief that, as novelist Rex Beach wrote, "the ignorant black man is no match for the educated white man," had begun to run its course. The anonymous mediocrities and yawning overdoses served up during the plague years in which Johnson held the title had risen and mercifully then vanished without a trace. Now one emerged called a "White Hope" for the same reason an aging lady of the streets applies rouge to her cheeks—to gussy up his credentials.

Jess Willard was an ordinary fighter, at best. He had had a recent series of uneven performances, including no-decision fights against fellow "White Hopes" Luther McCarty, Carl Morris, and Arthur Pelky, beaten George Rodel and Bull Young—who died as a result of a ponderous right hand cantilevered by Willard—and lost to the "White Heavyweight champion" Gunboat Smith.

Still, this Leviathan of a man was awesome, not for his record so much as for his size. Standing six-foot-six-and-one-half inches tall and almost as much in circumference at 250-plus pounds, Willard was the sort of man one would expect to meet at the top of a beanstalk. Hailing from a place just about an axle-greasing away from Pottowatamie, Kansas, he became known as "the Pottowatamie Giant." And he became Jack Johnson's next opponent.

This addition to the long list of so-called standard-bearers for the white man's crusade was one of the rawest recruits ever pressed into action for Armageddon. Twenty-seven before he ever saw a boxing glove and 29 before his first professional fight—that a ten-round loss to one Louis Fink in some one-horse town named Sapulpa, Oklahoma—Willard was derisively referred to as "Cowboy Jess," a reference to his previous life, where he had been a cow-puncher, rodeo rider, and plains teamster.

The year after he started, 1912, he determined on a course for himself—and, unbeknownst to him, the white race—when he visited Professor O'Connell's gym in Chicago "to take a gander" at Jack Johnson, then in training for a bout with Fireman Jim Flynn, a fight he would win easily in nine rounds. After Johnson had done some pulling of chest weights, he looked around and said, "Anybody heah want to do a little boxing?" Nobody responded to his call to arms and Johnson went over to where the big cowboy was standing. "Come on." "No," Willard replied, "I'd better not." Johnson tried to coax him. "Don't be afraid," he laughed, "I never hurt a green boy." "It isn't that," responded to Willard. "I mean to fight you someday, and I'd rather wait until I meet you in the ring." The flustered Johnson just looked the big kid over and then grinned, saying, "Say, if these White Hopes keep gettin' bigger I'll have to buy some stilts."

Willard watched Johnson work, knowing in his heart, as he put it, he "could whip him. He had cleverness, all right enough, but the whites of his eyes weren't clear. His left hand was fast as a flash, but a roll of fat dropped over his belt." Willard went home determined he could beat the man who had mastered all his white masters. And every time Willard read "about Johnson tucking away wine," he'd figure, "just one round less."

Finally that time came, not so much because Willard had earned it but because Johnson figured he was just another White Hope. And because promoter Jack Curley had promised he would pose "no threat." Curley also made other promises to induce Johnson into a Havana ring in defense of his championship, some he could keep and some he was in no position to keep. But Curley really didn't care; he was merely indulging in a promoter's prerogative, issuing illusory promissory notes in search of an event. He promised Johnson $35,000 as well as something about getting him a pardon from the United States government.

Johnson bought all of it, lock, stock, and pardon, and put his title on the line for the sixth time against this enormous but clumsy fighter, whom he thought so little of he barely trained.

Johnson entered the ring first, under a hot, blistering Havana sun blazing down on Havana's Oriental Park. It was apparent to all that he was out of shape. Not only was he no longer lean, but the 37-going-on-42-year-old champion was no longer the man-eater he once had been, mentally wearied from his travails with the law, and age and inactivity having taken a greater toll than any opponent ever had.

Promised first by Curley that his money would be forth-coming at the prefight weigh-in—which took place in the ring immediately before the fight—and then amended by Curley to read that it would be delivered to his wife, seated ringside, John-son reluctantly went on to the fight. The bell sounded and Wil-lard came out cautiously, throwing the first punch, a long left that penetrated Johnson's defenses, the first time any opponent had ever dared lead—or worse, land—on the great Jack Johnson. It was a portent of things to come.

As the bout wore on under the 103-degree-and-rising heat, Willard seemed to get stronger. And Johnson weaker. The enor-mous but clumsy opponent standing in front of Johnson contin-ued to bear in on the champion, using his long, 83-inch reach to get through what had heretofore been Johnson's proudest posses-sion, his defense. By the end of the tenth round Willard threw his long arm avuncularly around Johnson's shoulders, now sure that he couldn't be hurt and that the fight and the crown would ultimately be his.

As round after round passed, the sand began running out of Johnson's heavyweight hourglass. By the twenty-second, with Willard still as strong as he was in Round 1 and his wife still indicating Curley had not as yet made his promised visitation, Johnson sent one of his cornermen to "fetch Curley" and get his money. Then, he returned to the action at hand, action that saw Willard continue to press forward, continue to take Johnson's best, and continue to stalk the rapidly aging champion.

By the twenty-fifth Curley had finally made his way down from the box office to ringside, where he gave an envelope to Johnson's wife. After being informed personally by Curley between Rounds 25 and 26 that she had finally received the promised money, Johnson told the promoter, "Tell my wife I'm tiring . . . I wish you'd see her out," so sure was Johnson now that he was on the last leg of his eight-year reign as heavyweight champion.

Then came the fateful twenty-sixth. It started like most other rounds, with Willard swinging his poleaxe right. Johnson, feeling his strength ebbing, tried a last-ditch effort to dislodge his great bull of an opponent. After blocking Willard's right, he unleashed a fusillade of punches—a left, a right, another left and right, and still another series of lefts and rights—all driving Willard across the ring into Johnson's corner. Willard held up under the punishment, finishing the exchange in better shape than the now-exhausted Johnson, spent from his efforts. Willard surmised that the offensive outburst was the last, spasmodic gasp by an expiring champ, and, moving back toward the center of the ring, threw a powerful left to the body, followed by an overhand right with all of his 260 pounds behind the blow. Johnson tried to grab Willard to stay his fall, then slowly slipped beneath his bulk, falling full-length to the floor, his arms over his eyes, shading himself from the noonday sun, almost by instinct. Referee Jack Welsh tolled off the fateful "ten" and raised a white arm in victory.

The longest heavyweight title bout in Marquess of Queensberry history was over—along with dreaded reign of Jack Johnson. Almost as soon as Johnson was hauled erect by his cornermen, he mumbled between puffed lips, "It was a clean knockout and the best man won. It was not a matter of luck. I have no kick coming."

Within months, however, this spitfire would burn up with spite, and through the spontaneous combustion of pure fury and shame ignite into a "confession," one he wrote and sold to Nat Fleischer of *The Ring* magazine. He claimed that, as part of a pre-arranged agreement, he had agreed to lose between the tenth and twentieth rounds, but because of Willard's "poor performance" had had to wait until the twenty-sixth. It was a sad postscript to the shame of a man who had let his inner anger and arrogance consume him, but who was in the eyes of many the greatest heavyweight champion of all time.

Regardless of how he rationalized his loss, he had lost. That was all that mattered. He was now the ex-champion. The "Dark Ages" of boxing were over, at least in the minds of white America. Little did they know boxing was now on the threshold of something far greater: the "Golden Age of Boxing."